COLUMBUS

Felipe Fernández-Armesto has been a member of the Modern History faculty of Oxford University since 1983. He has also held appointments at Brown University and the University of Warwick. He now lives in Wassenaar, in The Netherlands.

ALSO BY FELIPE FERNÁNDEZ-ARMESTO

The Canary Islands After the Conquest

Before Columbus: Exploration and Colonization from the Mediterranean to the Atlantic, 1229–1492

The Spanish Armada: The Experience of War in 1588

Barcelona: A Thousand Years of the City's Past

Columbus

The Times Atlas of World Exploration (Editor)

Columbus on Himself

Edward Gibbon's Atlas of the World

The Times Guide to the Peoples of Europe (Editor)

Truth: A History and a Guide for the Perplexed

The European Opportunity (Editor)

The Global Opportunity (Editor)

The Times Illustrated History of Europe

Millennium: A History of the Last Thousand Years

Reformation (with Derek Wilson)

Reformations: A Radical Re-interpretation of Christianity and the World, 1500–2000

COLUMBUS

And the Conquest of the Impossible

Felipe Fernández-Armesto

**PHOENIX
PRESS**

5 UPPER SAINT MARTIN'S LANE
LONDON
WC2H 9EA

A PHOENIX PRESS PAPERBACK

First published in Great Britain
by Weidenfeld & Nicolson in 1974
This paperback edition published in 2000
by Phoenix Press,
a division of The Orion Publishing Group Ltd,
Orion House, 5 Upper St Martin's Lane,
London WC2H 9EA

© Felipe Fernández-Armesto 1974

A CIP catalogue record for this book
is available from the British Library.

Set by Selwood Systems, Midsomer Norton
Printed and bound in Italy by
Grafica Veneta S.p.A.

ISBN 1 84212 084 0

Contents

ILLUSTRATIONS

Between pages 82 and 83

11. One of Columbus's navigational aids: an astrolabe that belonged to the Viennese astronomer Georg Peuerbach, *c.* 1457. The problems of navigation were only incompletely solved at the time of Columbus's voyages. Many of the instruments available were clumsy to use and inaccurate. John II of Portugal summoned a commission of mathematical experts in 1484 and some of their findings were published in *Regimento do astrolabio e do quadrante* (*The Regiment of the Astrolabe*), a manual for the practical guidance of sailors.

12. Vasco da Gama: a portrait by a contemporary artist.

13. A modern view of the Virgin Islands, looking Westward from the west end of the island of Tortola.

14. The urn containing the ashes of Columbus at the Palazzo Tursi, Genoa. On it is the Genoese coat of arms.

Unless otherwise indicated all illustrations are courtesy of the Weidendfeld Archive.

Introduction

It delights me to think that this book – commissioned over a cocktail when I was twenty-one years old – is still worth re-publishing for readers interested in my work.

After writing it, I spent ten years at Oxford teaching courses based in part on texts by Columbus. Later, I edited and translated selections from those texts and wrote what has become the standard biography. In the meantime, my research projects explored related subjects in the history of exploration and cartography and led me to a series of new insights and discoveries.

As far as I know, the facts given in the book are all correct; and the original information it includes from research I had in hand when I wrote it – especially on the Mediterranean background of early Atlantic exploration, on the way Columbus's career was financed and on his role in devising early institutions for colonial society – has all been confirmed.

I owe readers, however, an explanation of how recent research modifies important matters of interpretation; the publishers have kindly allowed a few pages for this task.

First, the nature of the sources needs to be re-appraised. At the age of twenty-one, I felt that sources from Columbus's own hand and those of contemporaries could be relied on, if handled critically. In work I have published since 1986, I have taken an even more deeply sceptical approach. The document which inspired the first sentence of the present book was a map which is now discredited as a profiteer's forgery of the last century. The 'life' of Columbus previously attributed to his son must now be regarded as of doubtful authenticity. Not only are forgeries far more rife in Columbus's wake than I formerly allowed for: the genuine documents are more deviously warped by agendas of Columbus's own and his earliest editor's. What were once loosely categorised as lightly-edited versions of his shipboard reports and journals are really romantic and poetic passages of autobiography, most of which have been further distorted by editorial hands. The picture they yield should be understood less as a factual account of Columbus's experiences than as an opaque source of insights into his mercurial and egotistical state of mind. One effect of this discovery is to make it impossible to reconstruct the route of Columbus's first Atlantic crossing with any confidence.

Secondly, my understanding of what drove Columbus – if you like, what made him tick – has been transformed by long acquaintance with his work. I now see him as motivated primarily by none of the traditional range of self-perceptions represented in my early work: not by scientific curiosity or missionary zeal or messianism or material cupidity, but rather by social ambition. This weaver's son, who dreamed of self-transformation into Admiral of the Ocean Sea and founder of an aristocratic dynasty, might have tried any of the routes of self-aggrandisement common in his day: war or the church or seaborne exploration. He fixed on the last and made a remarkable success of it.

This re-evaluation also affects my picture of the sources of Columbus's thought. I once supposed, in conformity with the historical tradition, that he formed his plans as a result of reading books of geography. I now think his self-education in that discipline came after he had already conceived his ambitions through reading other kinds of literature: saints' lives and, above all, novels of chivalric romance, which were the late-medieval equivalent of station-bookstall pulp-fiction. Many of these works had a seaborne setting. Indeed, the deeds of knight-errants were enhanced at sea, where God's hand was peculiarly active and obvious in stirring or stilling the winds and waves, and where ships could be ridden like jennets. The usual plot was of a hero down on his luck or unjustly derogated, who took to sea, conquered an island and, if all went well, married a princess and became a ruler. That was the life-trajectory Columbus conceived for himself and followed, in practice, as closely as he could.

In consequence, the traditional debate over his intended destination no longer seems important to me. Although it remains true, as I argued in the book below, that he explicitly set off in 1492 on a presumed voyage to Asia, what really mattered to Columbus was not where he was going, but whether he would 'arrive' in a social sense. Hence the contradictions of the sources: he proposed at various a voyage in search of new islands, a transatlantic crossing of vague destination, a search for an unknown continent and a quick route to Asia, according to whom he was addressing. In his search for patronage he was prepared to argue for anything likely to appeal to his hearers: as long as he was allowed to make a voyage, and discover something, he didn't much care what it was.

He was inconsistent in everything except changeableness. In 1972, I was still a little under the influence of a traditional, legendary

Columbus-image of Columbus's own making, according to which he was a character of unswerving constancy of purpose and unwavering vision. In later work I set out to rebuild this adamantine Columbus in mercury and opal. I used in particular to overestimate his consistency in religion: I believed him to be motivated from an early stage of his planning by mysticism and millenarianism. We now know a great deal more about Columbus's intense religious life and his millenarian obsessions, thanks especially to Alain Milhou. It is a subject which deserves more prominence than I gave it in 1972. I now believe, however, that it was the product of a long conversion-experience, which grew on Columbus, as religion often grows on us, in consequence of what he perceived as his misfortunes. The evidence formerly thought to suggest that millenarianism influenced Columbus's first conception of his enterprise has evaporated on close scrutiny. His attitude to the peoples he encountered is best chronicled against his progressive religiosity: it was a dynamic process of increasing awareness, not the sudden unveiling of a pre-packaged set of perceptions depicted below.

I have also changed my mind about his methods of navigation. In 1972 I accepted, as most historians did, that Samuel Eliot Morison had exhausted the critical possibilities in this area and that Columbus navigated by dead reckoning. Work by other historians, especially Paul Adam and R. Laguarda Trias, makes this now seem an inadequate analysis. Columbus is best understood as a primitive celestial navigator. The instruments he took on board were just for show: he did not know how to use them. But he made crude readings of the hours of daylight and relied, until he became sufficiently practised, on printed tables to convert these observations into calculations of latitude.

I feel that one can now be more precise about the nature of Columbus's achievement than I was in 1972. I stand by everything about this which is said below. But it is worth stressing additionally that what Columbus discovered was a route from Europe to the New World and back which was previously unrecorded and which remained, with some modifications, the standard route throughout the age of sail. Strictly speaking, this was an achievement of 1493, not 1492, since Columbus's first outward route proved unsatisfactory and it was only on his second crossing that he made the best possible use of the Atlantic wind-system. World history is a matter of cultural transmissions at long range, which depend on explorers for route-finding. Columbus found routes which, for the first time and forever, established viable, commercially exploitable and durable links between hemispheres which then began to influence each other in re-shaping ways. Of these the most important was the exchange of biota, studied brilliantly in the work of A.W. Crosby: the divergent path evolution had previously followed, as species developed ever more variously from continent to continent, was replaced by convergence, as long-range navigation took life-forms to and fro between new environments.

Columbus's voyages were of enormous importance in other ways, too: in the history of cultural encounters, of Spanish imperialism, of the expansion of Christendom and of the mapping of the Atlantic winds, and in the projection of what we now call western civilization beyond its historic limits. But the creation of an Atlantic civilization, embracing both the ocean's shores, is a genuinely transcendent achievement. People say it would have happened anyway: but Columbus deserves personal credit or blame, because previous attempts to cross the Atlantic in central latitudes had all failed: they had been made against the wind – presumably because explorers were as anxious about getting home as anywhere else. By demonstrating the exploitability of following winds Columbus really did change the way people in Europe perceived the ocean.

Readers of this book who want to become up-to-date with the subject will find useful summaries of the existing state of knowledge in W.D. and C. Phillips, The Worlds of Christopher Columbus (Cambridge, 1992) and F. Fernández-Armesto, Columbus (London, 1996).

F.F.-A.
The Netherlands Institute for Advanced Study in the
Humanities and Social Sciences,
Wassenaar, 27th December, 1999

COLUMBUS

AND THE CONQUEST OF THE IMPOSSIBLE

A Spanish ship; woodcut of 1496.

A SELF-MADE MAN

Genove la Superba, 'Genoa the proud', the ancient maritime
city in which Columbus was born. An engraving from the
Nuremberg Chronicle of 1493.

THE STORY OF THE DISCOVERY of America really began when the idea of sailing across the western ocean for the first time in recorded history entered the sometimes febrile and always sensitively balanced brain of a clothier-turned-mariner named Christopher Columbus. How through his upbringing, reading and early travels his mind conceived and bore that idea is the pre-natal history of a whole hemisphere.

Columbus was raised in an atmosphere redolent with the smell of the sea and noisy with rumours of explorations nearly accomplished or more discoveries shortly to be made. His birth, on an uncertain date around the mid-turn of the fifteenth century, probably in 1451 or late in 1450, occurred in the middle of the period of the most intensive and wide-ranging navigation undertaken by Mediterranean men since Phoenician times. In particular, European knowledge and experience were unfolding like a map over two hitherto almost unknown areas: Africa, where an important part of Columbus's preparation would be gained, and the great ocean where his thoughts were eventually to rest and where his ambitions would be partly fulfilled and finally frustrated, the Ocean Sea, as men called it then, the Atlantic. At the same time, among scholars in Europe there was a vigorous upsurge of geographic speculation and theorising, in which Columbus read avidly and participated personally, accompanied by the re-discovery of old authorities and the writing of new ones.

Columbus's birthplace, Genoa, was not renowned for scholars and in the theoretical field contributed little to the geographical revolution of the fifteenth century. In other respects, however, it was the ideal location in which a future discoverer of America might spend his most impressionable years. For the life of Genoa flowed on the surface of the ocean: like the other Italian coastal city-states, she lived by trade and therefore by the sea. Genoa's position on the western side of the Italian peninsula separated her from the best-thumbed sources of traditional trade – the eastern Mediterranean ports where the spice-caravans from the Orient terminated – and placed her merchants at a disadvantage compared with those of her greatest rival, Venice. But she was correspondingly closer to those zones of still unrealised importance – West Africa, with its mysterious gold trade, and the unknown Atlantic.

The tradesmen of Genoa were daring entrepreneurs: they had to be, in the Middle Ages, to trade internationally, for the dangers to shipping were so much greater then than now, from pirates, storms and who-knew-what sea monsters and other preternatural perils. They were willing to travel, even to migrate, in the pursuance of their trade, and wasted little time in exploiting the areas where nature favoured them with easier access than the Venetians. While the latter, like valley sheep, grew fat – to judge from the Venetian style of portraiture – and lazy amid the lucre of the Levant, the Genoese, like mountain sheep, lived austere lives in merchant colonies quartered in the alien ports of the west. Records surviving from the Genoese community of Cadiz showed how they ploughed all their profit back into their enterprises and for most of the fifteenth century possessed little beside their bare homes, unornamented by more than the essentials in furniture, until by the end of the period this thriftiness had made them rich and enabled them to invest in jewels and carpets and indulge in luxuries.

In the third quarter of the thirteenth century Genoese ships passed between the pillars of Hercules into the Atlantic for the first time. Soon they were seeking havens as remote as Flanders and England, and a company of Genoese merchants, led by the Vivaldi brothers, undertook a remarkable pre-enactment of Columbus's own ideas by trying to sail 'to the regions of India by way of the Ocean Sea', in 1291, fully two hundred years before Columbus tried the same thing himself and discovered America in the process. The Genoese later charted parts of the African coast and the Canary Islands – another seed-plot of Columbus's future experience and ideas. But the dissemination of maps and sea-charts depicting the newly investigated coasts from the 1320s onwards meant that the Genoese monopoly of navigation in the area was doomed. An era was inaugurated of increasing international competition for the conquest, trade and exploitation of new lands.

By the time of Columbus's birth, this medieval space race, so to speak, was led by Portugal, another country which would play an important part in Columbus's intellectual formation and where he would for many years make his home, but there were many other contenders for the rewards of exploration. Frenchmen, Scandinavians and Spaniards had all struck into the Atlantic in search of new fisheries, booty, colonies and peoples to convert or enslave. Italian navigators had guided Portuguese emissaries and captains as they searched Africa for allies against the enemies of Christendom: the crescent of Islam, it must be remembered, still waxed over Spain, all North Africa and the Holy Land, while one of its horns protruded ominously towards Constantinople and the Mediterranean islands. The motives for the expansion of Christendom were as varied as the nations which engaged in it: fish to catch, trade to capture, slaves to master, lands to conquer and settle, allies to make, gold to gain, souls to save.

In the pursuit of all of these, the Portuguese were the most successful

MYTHICAL MONSTERS AT SEA

Medieval illustrators imagined the sea to be full of monsters which threatened their safety, and many old legends are based on these fantasies.

Top left and right Woodcuts of beasts at sea and on land, from Sebastian Münster's *Cosmographia universalis* (1544)

Above A monster being caught in a net: from the Nuremberg Chronicle (1493).

A selection of mythical monsters, some winged, from the *Buch der Natur*,
published in Augsburg (1475)

of the rivals with a spectacular record of discovery and settlement on the west coast of Africa. Columbus's Genoa heard of these exploits but it was in Lisbon itself and on the Portuguese sea-lanes that Columbus learned about them. In particular, Portuguese explorations up to the time of his birth contributed to his formation by destroying the fabric of superstition inherited from Arab authors, who had spread rumours about natural and supernatural factors that were supposed to make the unknown seas and tropic zones unnavigable.

Genoa, when Columbus was born there, was characterised by expansion and enterprise, while much of Italy seems to have been suffering from economic stagnation. Population was increasing under the influence of a rising birth-rate, which by the middle of the fifteenth century had recovered to a level it had not reached since the Black Death. A drain of migrants from the countryside to the town, which represented the triumph of the mercantile over the rural way of life in Genoa, together with immigration from further afield in Italy, France and Spain, helped to people the city with over a hundred thousand inhabitants by the end of the century. Money was more readily available than ever. About three years before Columbus's birth, the Genoese government had decreed the payment of all bills of exchange in gold – almost alone, it seemed, in Europe, Genoa was not suffering from a shortage of specie: no doubt Genoese interests in the gold trade of the Mahgrib and Spain account for this. The increase of available specie in Genoese markets caused an expansion of credit, and the banks, including the great, corporate state bank of San Giorgio for internal transactions, assured the facility and flow of trade.

The direction in which trade was increasing fastest – and the source too of an explanation of why Genoa was doing so singularly well economically among the states of Italy – was towards the expanding markets of the very zone to which Columbus, like so many of his countrymen, would be drawn, towards the Atlantic, to Portugal, Spain, the Atlantic archipelagos and northern Europe. Columbus would later receive material help from the Genoese communities settled in Lisbon, Seville and the Canary Islands.

It was into this world, Mediterranean in culture but linked to the Atlantic by a thread of gold and an expanse of brine, that Cristoforo Colombo, as he was then known, was born. The house where he was reared stood just outside the walls of Genoa, by the Porta Sant'Andrea. It became his family's house in 1455, within a few years of his birth. His father, Domenico Colombo, carried on the family business as a maker and marketer of woollen cloth, travelling by way of his occupation to and from Savona and, no doubt, about Liguria, but rarely taking to the sea. In this respect, however, Domenico was an uncharacteristic Genoese. If his younger sons, Giovanni and Giacomo, generally stayed

Christopher Columbus: a woodcut by Tobias Stimmer, after Paolo Giovio. This is a version of the oldest portrait of Columbus known to us, but even this was not published until 1577, many years after Columbus's death in 1506.

close to the familiar looms, the elder pair, Cristoforo and Bartolomeo, shared with most of the boys of Genoa an early fancy for the sea.

Nothing more is known of Columbus's antecedents, but it seems clear that his family was without social distinction. When late in life he had risen to prominence in the service of Spanish monarchs, jealous contemporaries would taunt him with the obscurity of his origin and suggest that his lowly blood incapacitated him for high office. Columbus's reactions were mixed. He might fling his detractors' accusations back in their faces, exulting in the humble background he had left behind him, or at times he might make egregious claims to a noble and seafaring lineage. In his jockeyings for rank, under the Castilian crown, for instance, he arrogated to himself a quite spurious coat of arms. These pretensions were too vague to be trustworthy, and are clearly psychologically explicable. On one occasion he boasted that he was 'not the first Admiral of my line': that must have been, to say the least, an overstatement, but it is unlikely that no one connected with a Genoese family such as the Colombi were should ever have taken to the sea. Perhaps the brine in Columbus's blood, if any there was, came from his mother's side of the family, about whom we know nothing. While it is possible that he had nautical ancestors, it is quite improbable that he was of Jewish blood or belonged to any of the various nationalities, other than the Genoese, which later writers have claimed for him.

Columbus's Hebraism has become one of the most tenacious of many popular misconceptions about him, although there is not a scruple of evidence to support it. The hypothesis was suggested by the fact that the only language (save Latin, in which we may be sure he was not reared) ever employed in Columbus's surviving writings is Spanish. Therefore, the argument runs, Spanish must have been his household tongue, and a circumstance which might explain the presence of a hispanophone family in Genoa is that they were converts from Judaism, who left Spain to escape the social disadvantages of their status. In fact, however, there is no reason why Columbus might not have learned his Spanish later in life and thereafter adopted it for his writings as did, for instance, his near-contemporary, the Emperor Charles v. He never indeed quite rid his Spanish of alienisms, but there was nothing Jewish about the lapses he made. As for the presumed supporting evidence of his Hebraism, it is true that he loved to use Biblical figures of speech about death, and was an enthusiastic reader of the Old as well as the New Testament. But as we shall see, his fantasies about the end of the world and preference for Sacred History were typical of both the man

and his times, appropriate to the complexion of Columbus's own character and shared by many of his contemporaries. The Doom-fraught
character of his teleology seems anyway more properly Christian than
Jewish. For the hypothesis that the mistress of his later years was a
Jewess, even less evidence exists than in his own case. Finally, it is
unthinkable in the Spain of his day that he would have escaped denun-
ciation by his numerous enemies, had his contemporaries harboured
any suspicions of the purity of his blood.

As for his more immediate origins, in his surviving writings
Columbus refers to neither of his parents; yet it seems that his mother
exerted some indefinable influence over him, since throughout life he
was much given to the use of maternal imagery. He shared, we know,
his father's devotional life, joining, in the company of his brother
Bartolomeo, a civic confraternity in Genoa, dedicated to the cult of St
Catharine. The nature of this guild was no doubt only partly pious and
it was characteristic of the confraternities of that period that they
should have some social or economic role as well, uniting men of the
same class or trade. Columbus maintained a tenuous contact with and a
marked affection for his family in Genoa throughout his life. From an
uncertain point in the mid-1470s, Bartolomeo was the companion of all
his adventures. Giacomo joined him in Spain when the older brothers
had found fame. Shortly after, in 1496, Columbus's young cousin,
Giannetto, was sent by the collateral Colombi to try, no doubt, to gain
some advantage from the patronage their fortunate relative disposed of,
now that he was the King of Spain's admiral. Columbus duly appointed
Giannetto to a command in the next expedition he mounted. In his
bequests to his son, Columbus subsequently made provision for the
Genoese branch of his family to be maintained in that city for ever in
their own house, 'since from Genoa I came and therein was I born'.

His pride in and love of his native city never deserted him. He loved
to profess himself Genoese-born, even when it became dangerous for
any foreigner to hold wealth or power in the Spanish empire and when
his enemies were using his alien provenance to poison his reputation.
He deposited money in the state bank of San Giorgio and made a
bequest to that institution, when he had become wealthy and famous,
so that the citizens' burden of taxation should be reduced. In April
1502, he wrote from Castile to the directors of the San Giorgio an
expression of sentiment which eloquently proves his enduring attach-
ment to the homeland he had not seen, by that time, for a generation's
span: after describing the position he had achieved, 'Sirs,' he declared,
'although my body wanders here, my heart is continually in Genoa.'

A sense of the humbleness of his circumstances, the deep but unobtrusive influence of his mother, and patriotism: these then were the earliest abiding impressions that the young Cristoforo Colombo acquired. But it was of course not long before he progressed from sensations to thoughts and from impressions to ideas. The ambition to be an explorer took form with the beginnings of the barely formal but intensely practical education he gradually acquired. In 1502, when the climax of his career was past and his health and fortunes were already in decline, he described in these words the formation of his ambition – his 'desire' or design as he called it:

> All the seas and coasts that have been sailed up to the present have I sailed. I have talked and lived with the learned – churchmen and laymen, Latins and Greeks, Jews and Moors and many others of other creeds – and to this design of mine I found Our Lord very favourable, and for its sake He gave me the spirit of understanding: in seafaring He over-endowed me; of astronomy He taught me sufficient, as of geometry and arithmetic, with invention in my soul and a draughtsman's hands. Over the years have I seen and studied books on every science: cosmography, history, chronicles and philosophy and other arts, whereby Our Lord opened to my understanding with His manifest hand that it was possible to navigate from here to the Indies.

His great idea was evidently a product of self-education. Like other religious men in a similar position, Columbus ascribed to God what was effectively his own role in educating himself. No doubt this weaver's son had little chance of formal schooling when he was small. He certainly never attended a University (his supposed place among the *alumni* of Pavia was an invention of his first biographer's). It is therefore not surprising that Columbus's mind suffered all the defects that a guideless and random absorption of knowledge can impart, like a ship at large upon a starless ocean. He had read extensively but not critically and acquired a mass of information but was never able to dispose of it to his best advantage. He would leap to bizarre conclusions on the flimsiest evidence, which a more balanced preparation might have taught him to eschew. He selected his reading matter not intellectually but obsessively, reading only what related to his own favourite theories, rejecting or distorting whatever failed to support his prejudices. His friend Andrés Bernáldez, the academic curate of Extremadura and historian of his own times, sized Columbus up as a man of great intellect but little education: that was not strictly accurate, for Columbus used his intellect to educate himself, teaching himself enough Latin to impress even the fastidious scholars at the Spanish and Portuguese Courts, mastering other languages not his own, preparing himself adequately to converse with the brilliant and the mighty, embarking on a literary career which for its sheer quantity became celebrated in his day and assembling a formidable body of authority that did credit to his powers of research in support of his idea of crossing the Ocean. But his self-schooling was vitiated by its fatal imbalance. It was partly a consequence of that imbalance that Columbus's idea became an obsession and possessed him more thoroughly as he grew older, until at last, as we shall see, it consumed him from within, bringing him successively to disappointment and virtual destruction.

The obsession originated in the elements of Columbus's education as he himself described them – the voyages of which he boasted and the reading of which he was so proud. We have Columbus's own word for it that the ambition to explore came to him with his first experience of the sea. 'From a very small age,' he wrote in 1502, 'I went sailing upon the sea and have continued to this day,' – he was then about fifty years old – 'which very occupation inclines all who follow it to wish to learn the secrets of the world.' His navigational experiences, that is, drew him as if blown by a wind and pulled by a current into the ocean of geographical speculation. To advance his search after the 'secrets of the world', he soon turned to books, but his youthful travels came first, analytically as well as in time.

The 'very small age' at which he took to sailing can no longer be determined. The first biography, attributed to Columbus's son Ferdinand reported that it was at fourteen years; however that may be, the boyhood voyages cannot have been extensive, and Columbus was in his twenties before he settled finally upon a nautical career. Throughout his teens he carded wool for his father and made business trips for him, and when the family moved away to the quieter sea town of Savona, Cristoforo went too. In 1472, he was still buying wool for the family enterprise, but he was growing restless and if he had not already made his first long voyage, was soon to do so. For it was probably about this time that he took ship for Tunis on an occasion which his own subsequent account has only served to obscure:

> It happened to me [he wrote] that King René [of Naples] sent me to Tunis to capture the galeass *Fernandina*, and when we had already reached the isle of St Peter off Sardinia ... the crew that went with me mutinied and determined to go no further with the expedition, except to

return to Marseilles. Seeing that I could not change their minds, unless
by some deception, I allowed their demand but reversed the ship's
compass; I made sail at night and the following day at daybreak we were
already within Cape Carthage, though they had all taken it for granted
that we were heading for Marseilles.

Now Columbus, though not at all a pathological liar, almost never told
quite the literal truth. He was committed to hyperbole by the enormity
of his pretensions and had to exaggerate his accounts of his deeds in
order to match his exaggerated claims. This relation of his Tunisian
voyage is unconvincing as it stands: he was too young and inexperi-
enced to captain an expedition, yet the ruse practised upon the mutineers sounds characteristic of his devious and inventive brain. Later, on
his voyages to America, he used not dissimilar methods to deceive his
crews. And it seems likely that Columbus, no doubt the ambitious and
eager one among the sailors, should side with his captain against the
mutineers and put into his head the idea of tampering with the
compass. The fact that Columbus repeated this story in 1495, so many
years after the event, also smacks of pride in a personal achievement.
We can be reasonably sure therefore that already on his first recorded
voyage Columbus was displaying promising qualities for the future.

For the next few years, most of his known travels were made in
Genoese ships. He visited Chios, where he gained his first experience of
a merchant-colony, such as he was later to try to set up in his own discoveries, and where he stored up many reminiscences to be drawn on
later for the sake of comparisons in his writings about the New World.
And in May 1476, he made what, as far as we know, was his first trip
into the Atlantic, shipping in an armed convoy, of the sort the Genoese
state periodically floated to trade in Portugal, Flanders and England,
and was cast ashore after his vessel sank in action off the Portuguese
coast. It seemed to Columbus, as he told the story to his son Ferdinand,
like a providential escape from death. Certainly it was pregnant with
consequences for the future. The castaway began a long period of
habitual residence in Portugal, and a lifetime of navigation on the
Atlantic.

Circumstances were now more favourable than ever before to the
progress of his exploring ambitions, and it is significant that henceforth
he begins to take an interest in the techniques of navigation and to note
distances and latitudes on his voyages. In February 1477, he shipped to
Iceland via Galway in Ireland and by his own account, which may be
the product of another exaggeration, a hundred leagues beyond; he

A contemporary map of Iceland, decorated with sea monsters. Iceland, the ancient
Thule, was an important port of call for traders from Lisbon and Bristol, and Columbus
sailed there in February 1477.

made an inaccurate reckoning of the latitude of his position and – what
is more important – noted that Iceland lay 'much beyond the limit of
the West': this perhaps suggests that the notion of sailing to the Orient
by way of the Atlantic was by now influencing his observations. But he
still had a number of voyages to make and a great deal of reading to do
before he could work out a plan. Living now at Lisbon, he formed a
natural connexion with the Genoese community. In particular, the
Centurione family, whose Genoese branch were important merchant
bankers, befriended him and gave him employment – Columbus never
forgot their kindness to him. He was soon employed in a position of
trust, and it was in the Centurione interest that he made his first trip
into the Atlantic archipelagos in 1478 to buy sugar in Madeira for deliv-
ery in Genoa. As a business deal, the trip proved a failure but it gave
Columbus his first chance to observe the trade winds that eventually
were to help him to America, to deal in a product he later introduced
into the New World and to make the acquaintance of a different, more
permanent and settled type of colonial community than he had seen in
Chios. Finally, the expedition brought him into contact with one of the

An impression of Portugal, from the Nuremberg Chronicle. Columbus made Lisbon his
base after landing there in the autumn of 1478, and took advantage of the lively
intellectual climate there. Among the Portuguese, he could study navigation and the
various geographical works in Latin, Portuguese and Castilian which could advance his
career of exploration and discovery.

three archipelagos – the Madeira group, the Canaries and the Azores –
that were to play vital roles in the success of his transatlantic voyages.

At about this time, he gained an unrivalled opportunity to amplify
this inchoate acquaintance when he met and married in Lisbon Donha
Felipa Moniz, who was closely related to, and probably the daughter of,
one of the first colonisers of Madeira, lord of the neighbouring island of
Porto Santo. This marriage to a lady of noble rank shows that the
Centurione connexion had amounted to a considerable social advance
for Columbus, and one suspects that it cannot have been by coincidence that he wooed and won a wife so closely linked with the way of

life Columbus was marking out for himself – the way of Atlantic exploration. Donha Felipa, of whose life almost no record has survived,
seems to have exercised no personal influence over her husband. It was
probably in 1481 that she bore him his only legitimate son, who was no
doubt christened Diogo after the Portuguese fashion but whose name
always appears as Diego, following Castilian orthography. She did not
long survive the birth. But her indirect importance to Columbus was
enormous: she made his social rise secure, and according to Ferdinand
Columbus, she and her mother introduced the future explorer to her
family's navigational records and charts. The content of these documents is no longer ascertainable, but they must have formed a valuable
supplement to the geographic lore which – as we shall see in a moment
– Columbus was busily imbibing at the time.

During these years he certainly sailed among the known Atlantic
islands, resided on Madeira for a time and probably went to live in the
Canary Islands. There is no definite evidence, but a persistent local tradition links him with the island of Gomera, almost the westernmost
point of the known world and certainly the westernmost site of an adequate harbour for an ocean crossing. If we are right to believe that
Columbus was already contemplating the passage of the Atlantic, and
indeed had been so since 1477 at the latest, it is highly probable that he
would wish to make observations in Gomera. Moreover, as he formu-
lated his plans for the projected crossing, the Canary Islands occupied a
pivotal position in them; it is most unlikely that Columbus would have
ascribed this central importance to the Canaries without the benefit of
prolonged acquaintance with them and at least some knowledge of prevailing winds. As we shall see, it was his inclusion of a Canarian stage
that distinguished his own project from all previous plans for further
exploration of the Atlantic, and precisely because of the nature of the
winds that his own efforts were to enjoy a measure of success where
earlier endeavours had failed.

The last routes he beat while still formulating his idea were down the
coast of Africa on the track traditionally explored by the Portuguese
since Prince Henry the Navigator. The usefulness of these trips, in
which Columbus penetrated to the latitude of the Gold Coast and
visited the fortress the Portuguese erected there in 1481, was manifold:
in the first place, Columbus could practise the hard art of reading latitudes (though he frequently made mistakes) over a route where the
Portuguese king had already sent astronomers to make readings that
would serve as a check for Columbus's own calculations. Secondly, he
could test his own theory of the value of a degree in miles – an essential

factor in calculating the breadth of ocean he would have to traverse in his prospective crossing of the Atlantic. Thirdly, Columbus could familiarise himself with conditions in the latitudes he expected to have to explore. Finally, he could improve his own mastery of the business of seamanship and his knowledge of the 'secrets of the world'.

As far as it was the product of experience, Columbus's intellectual formation and more particularly the creation of his idea of transnavigating the Ocean Sea, was thus complete by the early 1480s. But his education was not merely a matter of learning from voyages. It had a less practical, a more academic side too. We do not know when Columbus began to read intensively in geographical authorities, but it seems clear that it was during his time in Lisbon that circumstances most favoured the start of his perusals. Even before he became acquainted with the documents and charts in the possession of his wife's family, he had been reunited with his brother Bartolomeo, who, sharing the other's nautical bent, but following it through a somewhat less obtuse angle, had gone to Lisbon to learn and pursue the new but rapidly expanding trade of cartographer.

Cristoforo – or Christovao, as he had become in the Portuguese rendering – was from his own point of view interested in the same trade and became highly skilled at it – at the height of his career he was able to map a coastline as he followed it, more accurately than almost any of his contemporaries. At times, particularly after his wife's death, while he was travelling in Portugal and Spain, trying to arouse support for his plan to cross the Atlantic, Columbus would find his brother's business a useful sideline, purveying maps and other works of geographical interest: more than one observer described him as a bookseller. Meanwhile, Bartolomeo and Columbus helped each other with their cartographical interests and pored over tomes of cosmographic wisdom; underlining and annotating in the margins anything that might bear on the great idea. At this stage the two brothers seem to have been equally enthusiastic about the westward voyage, so that it could perhaps be said to have been jointly their idea. But the quality of Columbus's enthusiasm, if it was not already more intense, rapidly became so. The project never had for Bartolomeo the obsessive nature it came to bear within his brother.

The brothers' books were collected by Columbus's son Ferdinand, and today are for the most part preserved in the Chapter Library of Seville Cathedral, which houses the explorer's great tomb. Thus the remains of Columbus's body lie close to the remnants of his mind, the books whose learning his brain absorbed and the annotations he and Bartolomeo scrawled in the margins in Spanish and Latin with crabbed and almost indistinguishable hands. There were at least five authorities whose works Columbus knew at first hand and who contributed to the germ of his theory. The first of these was Ptolemy's *Geography*. Re-discovered by western scholars earlier in the fifteenth century, this second-century Alexandrian compendium re-united much classical learning in what today would be thought a particularly unscholarly fashion. In Columbus's day, however, especially in Italy and Portugal, where Ptolemy had enjoyed his longest and widest currency, the authority of the *Geography* was thought superior to that of all other texts. At Ptolemy's remote hand, Columbus learned and accepted some items of information fundamental to the elaboration of his plans for crossing the Atlantic: in the first place, that the world was a perfect sphere – an inaccurate observation, but one which for the time being served the would-be explorer's purpose. Secondly, Ptolemy taught that the known world extended in a continuous land-mass from the western extremities of Europe to the easternmost limit of Asia and that between the two points lay an intervening ocean: from this Columbus was able to conclude that it was theoretically possible to pass from Europe to Asia across the Atlantic. The practicability of such an endeavour would depend on the distance involved. The last point on which Ptolemy's lore coincided with Columbus's theories was that to the south of the known world existed unknown lands – depending on the latitude Columbus might select for his oceanic crossing, this information could have an important bearing on a controversy that was shortly to convulse some of the Old World's finest brains, the question, that is, of whether it was possible for Columbus to discover any substantial new lands *en route* for the Orient. Furthermore, as most readers understood him, Ptolemy blocked the eastern route to India with hypothetical lands, enclosing the Indian Ocean.

It was precisely, however, on the matter of the viability of his scheme that Columbus was compelled to reject the authority of Ptolemy, because it included two points which, if correct would constitute insuperable obstacles to the execution of his plan. In Ptolemy's opinion, which most of Columbus's contemporaries shared, the known world occupied exactly half the circumference of the globe. Though Ptolemy allowed that the unknown Orient might extend beyond that point, Columbus would probably have the equivalent of nearly 180 degrees of ocean to traverse – an amount that must have equalled a distance beyond the range of any vessel of the day, especially on the relatively southerly latitudes Columbus intended to use for his crossing. Moreover, Ptolemy's calculation of the length of the earth's circumference, though probably not far from the true figure, was too great for Columbus's taste; for the Alexandrian's reckoning involved a somewhat hazardous under-estimate of the length of a degree on the surface of the world at 60⅔ Roman miles. This was still too much for Columbus. Since the larger the circumference of the globe, and the greater the length of a degree, the longer and less practicable his projected voyage, Columbus felt obliged to dismiss the Ptolemaic tradition on these matters and search other texts for indications of a shorter journey. Columbus's attitude to Ptolemy is a curious indication of how his mind worked and of the problems of scientific investigation at a time when experiment was beginning to rival tradition as a source of scientific authority. Columbus had a profound respect for the texts; as would be natural in a self-educated man, he probably felt a certain awe in their presence. But he knew that they could not satisfy his longing to know the 'secrets of the world'; later, whenever from his own experience he was able to disprove something Ptolemy had said, he would gleefully exult and had already taken pride in being a 'witness' to the fact that the tropic zones were habitable, on his voyage to the Gold Coast in the early 1480s. On the other hand, the study and knowledge of the texts and the acceptance of the authority even of Ptolemy, when it lent itself to Columbus's purposes, were seminal factors in the emergence of his ideas.

Columbus found a partial corrective to Ptolemy in the travels to the limits of Asia described by *The Book of Marco Polo*. It must be remembered that Marco Polo's text, by Columbus's time, was very old and much-perused, but that its authority was a matter of quite acerbic controversy. It was, it seems, among scholars in Italy and southern Germany that the departed Venetian traveller was most cordially trusted, while in other areas and among more traditional scholars his book was regarded with scepticism. Medieval men had been taken in by too many fables of untold wealth and unseen prodigies of nature in the East to give ready credence to a tale as full of marvels as Marco Polo's. It was not the sort of authority that Columbus would be advised to rely on when arguing the merits of his plan, but he was always uncritical in his selection of texts and found Marco Polo especially serviceable in three ways: to begin with, Columbus reckoned that Polo's travels in Asia must have taken him well beyond what Ptolemy had reckoned the furthest limit of Asia – this in itself would whittle down Ptolemy's unnavigably large ocean. Moreover, he made a special note of Polo's report of no less than 1,378 islands off the coast of Asia – no doubt Columbus thought that he might therefore make land before completing the long crossing. Finally, Marco Polo had reported, fifteen hundred miles out from China, the gilded, gardened, watered island of Cipangu. This was the first, and really remarkably reliable, notice to reach Europe of the existence of Japan, but because it was uncorroborated, it was a matter of doubt. Polo had misreckoned its distance from China and given no adequate indication of its whereabouts. Nevertheless, Columbus snatched at Cipangu like a golden straw in the midst of the Ocean Sea. He firmly relied, despite doubts as to its location and very existence, on the hope of finding Cipangu during his Atlantic crossing and breaking his journey there. As we shall have many occasions to confirm, Columbus was made of the quintessence of wishful thinking, and never allowed facts to stand in the way of theories.

His theories found their most formidable body of support in one of the first and greatest new geographic works of the fifteenth century, written under the shadow of the re-discovered Ptolemy, albeit with heavier reliance upon Pliny and Roger Bacon, by Pierre d'Ailly, the reforming Cardinal of Tournai. His *Description of the World* was Columbus's favourite reading, to which he returned over and over again until he must have known its contents thoroughly. D'Ailly's importance for him was that he shared or rather pre-empted Columbus's belief that the distance by sea between the extremities of the known world was relatively narrow, and introduced Columbus to Greek and Arabic sources, almost certainly previously unknown to him, of the same opinion. Above all, d'Ailly acquainted Columbus with Aristotle's observation that it was but a short way by sea from India to Spain: the learned Cardinal thought the journey could be accomplished *paucis diebus*, in a few days. And he also made Columbus aware of the computations of Alfraganus, as the name of the Islamic geographer al-Farghani was rendered in the West, which included the estimation of a degree at 56⅔ miles. Naturally, Columbus leaped at this apparently small figure, which he could use further to reduce the size of the globe in his own plans and so shorten his prospective voyage in conviction if not in fact. But again Columbus's uncritical assimilation of knowledge led him into a fantastic labyrinth of error. Alfraganus had been working in Arabic miles – in reality his estimate of the size of a degree was even greater than Ptolemy's – but Columbus insisted on treating the Arab's figures as though they were expressed in Roman miles, for the convenience of his own theory.

One of Columbus's Latin postils to d'Ailly's book shows how he attempted to corroborate experimentally his own conclusions about the measurement of a degree by comparing his calculations of distance traversed with the Portuguese royal astronomer's readings of latitude as he sailed down the West African coast:

Note that often when navigating from Lisbon to the south of Guinea, I have noted with diligence the distance [*viam*] travelled after the custom of sailors and mariners and then have taken the altitude of the sun with a quadrant and other instruments several times and found that my figures agree with those of Alfraganus, namely that a degree corresponds to 56⅔ miles ... therefore we may say that the circumference of the earth at the equator is 20,400 miles long. The same was found by Master Joseph, physician and astronomer, and many others, whom the most serene king of Portugal had sent expressly for the purpose.

Unfortunately, there were still at that time no scientific means of recording distance (the custom of 'sailors and mariners' was simply to make an experienced guess) nor had any reliable way been devised of reading latitude at sea. Under such conditions, not even Master Joseph could check Alfraganus's findings. To our certain knowledge neither he nor Columbus ever made a reading of latitude at sea that was even roughly right.

Columbus abstracted one more item from d'Ailly and stored it away for future reference: that the earthly paradise was located at the eastern extremity of Asia was a commonplace among men of the time, though occasional authors could be found to dispute it. It followed, however, if the common opinion was true, that that delicious place might lie near Columbus's projected track, though d'Ailly added the point that it was far removed from any humanly habitable land.

Alongside Ptolemy, Marco Polo and d'Ailly, three other sources in Columbus's library were formative influences upon his geographic ideas, but none of them really contributed to the development of his plan to cross the ocean. The scriptures had very little influence, in a geographic sense, on Columbus's plans until he had made many discoveries and so came to appreciate the supposed significance of the 'prophecies' of his activities that he culled from the psalms, prophets and gospels. At first, he appears only to have considered the statement in the apocryphal prophet Esdras (to which it was probably d'Ailly who drew his attention) that 'Six parts of the earth' are dry land. From this he deduced that Ptolemy's estimate of the extent of the known world was inadequate. The *Natural History* of Pliny, the oldest Western geographic text in continuous use, gave him a broad grounding in the commonly accepted fundamentals of his subject and helped to excite his expectations of more undiscovered islands in the Atlantic. Lastly, the *Universal History* of Aeneas Sylvius Piccolomini, who had been Pope under the name Pius ii, acquainted him with the controversy among scholars over the possible existence of an unknown continent. Pius's doubts on the subject help to show the dichotomy of thinking which the discovery of unknown texts of classical learning, together with the growth of scientific approach, imposed upon scholars in the mid-fifteenth century, whose schooling had been in the traditions of medieval Christian science with its heavy reliance upon accepted authority. Pius reviews all the evidence of unknown continents and appears inclined to accept it, but then stops short to point out that a Christian should believe that there is only one fully emerged, continuous land-mass, comprising Asia, Africa and Europe and that all the rest is covered, save for the few islands, by sea. The authority for this was Augustine's insistence that there can be no 'antipodes' or unknown habitable continent, because of the evangelic doctrine that Christ's word had been preached by the Apostles throughout the world. The same arguments, and the same tangle of empirical, classical and scriptural or patristic authority was soon to characterise scholarly discussion of Columbus's plans and achievements.

Beyond the books in his library, only two other written sources made a major contribution to those plans. Columbus can have known the work of Marinus of Tyre only through Ptolemy, but it provided him with an alternative – and more generous – estimate of the extent of the known world than Ptolemy's, and hence a smaller assessment of the size of the Ocean. And to all his book-learning, Columbus was able to add two letters, almost exactly alike in content, written by the celebrated Florentine physician and astronomer Paolo Toscanelli. Toscanelli was one of a number of scholars who came independently to conclusions similar to Columbus's, using much the same sources at roughly the same time, about the possibility of crossing the Ocean Sea. Toscanelli was concerned rather with theoretical possibilities than the practical problems involved – he showed no concern for winds and currents or favourable latitude or even the sailing capacities of the available vessels; he was merely bent on demonstrating that the way to 'the lands of spices' and concretely to Cipangu and Cathay did not involve insuperable distances of ocean. He had been consulted on these matters by an astronomically inclined canon of Lisbon named Fernão Martins in 1474, with the object of interesting the King of Portugal in a more economical route to the Orient than the tiresome voyage along the coasts of Africa, which, after half a century of trying, the Portuguese had still not accomplished. Toscanelli and Martins believed that other, quite mythical islands apart from Cipangu would be encountered in the Atlantic on the way to the East to help break the journey. On learning

of Toscanelli's opinion, Columbus canvassed it further, probably
towards the end of the 1470s, receiving in reply to his enquiry a
recapitulation of the Florentine's correspondence with Martins.

When he had inwardly digested Toscanelli's letters and processed
them mentally with the fruits of all his other reading and the experience
of his travels, Columbus's intellectual formation, as far as it touched the
great idea that henceforth would rule his life, was complete. His task
now was to make that idea reality.

2

A DIVINELY CREATED OPPORTUNITY

A ship in use at the time of Columbus: illustrated in the
Nuremberg Chronicle.

THE HEAD THAT HOUSED Columbus's great plans was marked by strong, ruddy features, set with clear blue eyes, tufted with thick red hair and held high on a frame of more than average size. Its bearer was loquacious and self-laudatory. His manner and speech exuded ambition. He was pre-disposed to success, unresponsive to setbacks and blind to any obstacle, of however incontestably material a nature, that might lie in his path. He had a deep conviction of self-righteousness and the unlimited capacity for self-deception that usually accompanies that quality. He was intensely religious, and his religion was strongly providential. Those whom he met he either infuriated or entranced. Through the laborious preparations in the 1480s for his Atlantic voyage, he would need all his powers of persuasion, gifts of

Columbus the mariner, 'called the Genoese', with astrolabe in hand in 1493: this engraving by Thevet is later in date.

presence and unremitting loyalty to his own genius, before in 1492 the longed-for journey could be made – and a second career commenced of bitterness and disillusionment more taxing even than the first, amid the semblance of success.

To bring his Atlantic plans down from the clouds, and lay them on the face of the ocean, Columbus had to find the means to mount an expedition and a patron powerful enough, in the event of success, to guarantee him the benefit of the fruits of his enterprise. For both these purposes it was necessary to canvass scholarly opinion in support of the geographical theory that was the nub of his idea.

The fate of the projected ocean crossing hung not only on the navigability of the possible distance involved but also on the profitability of the lands that lay on the further shore. For most of the time he spent making his plans, there seems little doubt that Columbus expected to find the 'Indias ͜ Indies across the Atlantic – that is, the easternmost regions of Asia, bordering India and including Cathay, Cipangu and the islands mentioned by Marco Polo. This was at once the least credible and most attractive part of his scheme: attractive, because a short route to the Orient, and the gold and spices believed to abound there, was among the most cordial aspirations of all the later medieval navigators. India was the gilded butterfly caught in their dreams in a net of ship's rigging. But the likelihood that Asia lay at a navigable distance across the Ocean seemed hopelessly unpromising to most scholars. As we have seen, Pierre d'Ailly popularised the notion early in the fifteenth century in a work that was much read in Columbus's day. Pietro Paolo Toscanelli believed in it. Afonso v of Portugal is known to have been considering the possibility at the very moment when Columbus was first fortuitously thrown up by shipwreck on his shores. There was also a group of scholars in Central Germany who favoured the theory of a narrow sea between India and Europe. It was there, in the year of Columbus's first voyage, that Martin Behaim produced his spherical map or 'globe' of the world, depicting a straitened Atlantic and featuring Cipangu prominently in its midst, while shortly afterwards his colleague, the humanist physician and traveller Hieronymus Münzer, in apparent ignorance of Columbus's activities, wrote to the King of Portugal urging him to attempt a westward crossing to the spice-lands. All these, however, were isolated instances of informed opinion coinciding with Columbus: the great weight of authority was immutably opposed to his notions of a diminutive earth, an exaggeratedly extended land-mass and a narrow Atlantic, and hence to the chances of a western route to Asia.

It was possible, however, to favour further attempts at Atlantic exploration while doubting whether Asia could lie accessibly close to hand. Europe had for centuries been alive with rumours of undiscovered Atlantic islands, and hopes which had been fed by the discovery of the archipelagos that lay off the coast of Africa. The most tenacious myths concerned the island of Antilia or of the Seven Cities, supposedly colonised by fugitives from Lusitania at the time of the Moorish conquest; St Brendan's Isle, the rumoured refuge of the fabled saint; the Isle of Brasil; the Hesperides mentioned by Homer; the habitations of the Amazons and the lands whither St Ursula and her fugitive virgins set out on their escape from pagan rapists. Some of these notional lands floated on assertions by the reputable old authorities Pliny and Isidore of Seville, that numerous islands existed in the ocean, while others were mere nephelococcygias, cuckoo-lands founded in the clouds out of the hallucinations of credulous seamen. Yet to contemporaries at the close of the Middle Ages the prospects that some or all of them really existed seemed undeniably good, in view of the large numbers of islands discovered in their supposed vicinity. Toscanelli thought that the voyage to Cipangu could be broken at the island of Antilia. The 'Antilles', Brazil, 'the Amazon' and St Ursula all contributed to the nomenclature of the New World.

According to his son, Columbus believed that even if he did not find Asia, his changes of striking one or more of the undiscovered islands were good. Certainly, other voyages were made into the mid-Atlantic, though without any success, in search of such islands both in Columbus's own time and for centuries afterwards, including the expedition of Fernão Dulmo in 1487 from Terceira in the Azores, which has provoked speculation that this voyage also was intended to find a western route to Asia. While Columbus was preparing his plans, he assiduously assembled empirical evidence of more land in the Atlantic. Some of this, he clearly thought, pointed to Asia, such as the flat-faced castaways whom he observed in Ireland and the oriental-looking corpses cast up in the Azores, while other indications – exotic flotsam and driftwood – were neutral and might have come from Asia or other unknown lands indifferently. But if Columbus ever entertained the possibility of making other landfalls in the course of his projected Atlantic crossing, it was the hope of reaching Asia that was most prominent in his mind. Merely to undertake another voyage in search of Atlantic islands, which might well prove unprofitable and would have little commercial or strategic importance, was not a proposal calculated to attract much patronage to his cause.

eloquence and ambition impressed the King, who extended him his lasting regard, but no help. The cosmographical committee dismissed his suit, apparently because they disbelieved in the existence of Cipangu. It was said later that Columbus had demanded excessive rewards in the event of success and that this was the cause of his dismissal, but the probability is that he requested only ennoblement – a cheap commodity to a king – and the guarantee of a share in the profits of the route and regions he would discover. No such price would have been too great for the Portuguese monarch to pay for a short route to Asia. Columbus's attempts to obtain King John's support were vitiated rather by the improbability of his plan than by the importunity of his demands.

From this disappointment in Portugal, Columbus for most of the next seven years transferred his frustrations to the neighbouring kingdom of Castile, loosely known as Spain since the joining of the Castilian and Aragonese crowns in the persons of King Ferdinand and Queen Isabella. If Castile had lagged behind Portugal in the race for new territories in which to expand, it had been for want not of will but of means. The Castilian kings had disputed the liberties of the Portuguese in Africa and the Atlantic islands since the 1340s, when both had claimed rights of conquest in the Canaries before the court of Pope Clement VI. On that occasion, the Pope had pre-empted both rivals by granting away the perquisites himself. From early in the fifteenth century Castilian jurists had evolved an argument which attributed rights of conquest in Africa to their own sovereign, by virtue of the supposed descent of the regality of the Visigothic rulers of all Spain, together with their rights against the Moors, through the line of the monarchs of Castile. Since the accession of Ferdinand and Isabella, to Castilian aspirations of expansion had been added Aragonese concern with the eastern Mediterranean and the trade-routes to the Orient. The sense of an impending struggle between Christendom and Islam, which had been gaining force gradually throughout the century, was particularly strong in Spain, the land of secular conflict with the Moors and more recent involvements against the Turks. Men in King Ferdinand's own circle nourished millennial fantasies of their master's conquest of Jerusalem in a final struggle that would bring the old prophecies of a last emperor of the world to fulfilment. At the same time, the Spanish monarchs were bent on the extinction of the surviving Moorish realm on Spanish soil – the kingdom of Granada – but were anxious not to cut themselves off from the North African gold trade which traditionally passed through Granada into their own hands. On a more pedestrian level, Spanish industry, commerce and shipping were enjoying an abundant period which added new urgency to the search for trade-routes and exotic marts. Finally, competition at all levels between Spain and Portugal had rarely been more intense than now, for the war in which Afonso v had sought to wrest the very crown of Castile from Isabella's grasp had ended only in 1479. The two realms had then come to an agreement whereby future spheres of expansion were to be partitioned – the Canary Islands, including any still undiscovered, with a portion of the African coast immediately opposite them, were to belong to Castile, while the rest of mainland Africa would be specifically the prey of Portugal. But no agreement could be definitive in the unstable ambiance which then prevailed, and by 1482, during marriage negotiations between the two dynasties, the terms were in the melting-pot again.

It was therefore natural that Columbus should turn from Portugal to Spain in his search for patronage. Furthermore, Ferdinand and Isabella were not the only protectors his new homeland might offer, and Columbus spent his first year in their realms forming slightly more modest connexions. Overseas expansion was not in Castile, as it was in Portugal, a long-established activity thoroughly controlled by the Crown. It was open to any Castilian subject who possessed the means and motive to take some ships on a slaving *razzia*, capture a Berber town, trade illicitly in Portuguese Guinea, conquer a Canary Island or invade the kingdom of Granada – or, if he so wished, attempt to sail to the Indies. Enterprises such as Columbus proposed added the lustre of glory to commercial advantage, and neither of these features was beneath the dignity of a typical Spanish grandee of the day. In particular, the Count of Medina Celi had invested handsomely in mercantile marine ventures, and had a traditional family connexion with Castilian expansion in the Canary Islands, while the Duke of Medina Sidonia was interested in taking part in the conquest of the Canaries and investing in the sugar trade. It was to these potential sources of help that Columbus addressed his first appeals. His proposal at this stage was for a strictly commercial voyage to the Indies in no more than four caravels. His plan was favourably received and Medina Celi apparently maintained him for some time, but the noblemen seem to have felt that the project was of such magnitude as to require royal approbation. A trip to the Indies would necessarily involve far more than commercial considerations and raise the question of the sovereignty of the lands visited, with negotiations in Portugal, no doubt, and supplications to the Pope.

Columbus had therefore to direct his pleas to the monarchs in person. But the institutions of the Spanish Crown were ponderous, audiences hard to obtain and the times unpropitious for supplications to the hard-pressed and penurious sovereigns. While Columbus set up a temporary home for himself at Córdoba, the ancient capital of the Spanish Caliphs, on the upper Guadalquivir, Ferdinand and Isabella were preoccupied with the recovery of the last Moorish strongholds in Spain. The task was daunting more from a financial aspect than from a military one, but while the war went on, it was clear that the monarchs would have no resources to spare for exploring. When Columbus at last bowed those russet curls towards their throne at his first audience with them in Córdoba in May 1486, their interest in the project was only potential. Ferdinand and Isabella would consider their decision but not hurry it.

Columbus must have already had friends and agents at Court, for he had obtained a private audience at which to expound his plans. At about this time he became associated with a group of Isabella's ministers whose interest in overseas expansion was already notorious and who included Alonso de Quintanilla, the presiding intellect of the conquest of the Canaries, and Francesco Pinelo, the Genoese financier and fund-raiser for the monarchs' projects. Only after years of effort would this nucleus of partisans grow to preponderance at Court. Columbus's audience marked a signal advance in the maturing of his plans, for though he seemed to make little impression on Kind Ferdinand, he won Isabella's permanent sympathy. Ferdinand habitually showed reserve wherever his wife bestowed favour – whether from policy or for personal reasons is not fully clear. Though neither the King nor the Queen understood much of astronomy or navigation, the King may have been more alert to the deficits of Columbus's reasoning than his spouse, while the Queen no doubt found the foreigner's religious fervour endearing.

In any event his friends' insistence and Isabella's favour obtained for Columbus the chance to put his case to a new committee of experts, less specialised and less summary than the tribunal which had already scorned him in Portugal. The commission made little progress under the presidency of Hernando de Talavera, whose radical views on other matters – for he opposed the Inquisition, favoured leniency towards the Jews and Moors and enthusiastically subscribed the conquest of the Canaries – could not be extended to include belief in anything as unlikely as a narrow sea to Asia or as unorthodox as the antipodes. He and his colleagues adjourned at the end of the year without reaching any conclusion. But the general feeling of the members was apparently insuperably opposed to giving credence to Columbus's ideas. The explorer was kept pendant on a thread of uncertainty for more than a year, sustained by occasional *pourboires* from the monarchs and the hospitality of his friends, until he altogether lost patience and decided to turn elsewhere for aid.

Late in 1486, Columbus had left Córdoba for Salamanca to accompany the Court and continue grappling with the Talavera committee. It is probable however that while still in the southern city he formed two associations that were to influence him in a way that deserves our attention. No mistress ever rivalled his own schemes in Columbus's affections; his plans for crossing the Atlantic obsessed him so exclusively that romance played a smaller role in his life than in most other men's. Later in life he affected the dress of a cenobite and even now seemed to favour the company of friars as much as that of women. Yet his passions were susceptible, and it was not long before an intrigue with a woman named Beatriz Enriquez de Haraña, of a family of carpenters and butchers in Córdoba, turned into a stable and enduring relationship. Columbus never married this women whose station in life was too far beneath his own, but always behaved responsibly and affectionately towards her. In one of his last memoranda to his legitimate son, he reminded him 'Take Beatriz Enriquez in your charge for love of me, as attentively as you would your own mother. See that she gets from you 10,000 *maravedís* a year, beyond her income from her meat business in Córdoba.' She bore Columbus a son, Ferdinand, who accompanied his father later to the New World, wrote an account of their journey and became one of the most famous men of letters of his time. Columbus was also insistent upon Ferdinand's dignity, writing to his legitimate son, 'Advise your brother as the elder son should to the younger. He is the only brother you have and may our Lord be praised that he is just such as you need; for he has turned out to be of very great learning.'

Beatriz Enriquez was probably not Columbus's only amorous encounter in Córdoba, for there he may have met a lady with whom he had no definite affair that we know of but an association which excited rumour. Beatriz de Bobadilla was one of the most beautiful and cruel women in Castile. From an involvement with the King himself, she had gone to the conquest of the Canaries in 1481 as the wife of the *conquistador* Hernán Peraza, lord of the island of Gomera. When he was murdered by rebellious natives, Beatriz became mistress of the island in her own right, suppressing the rebellion bloodily and enslaving many of the islanders. Later, after her amorous brush with Columbus, she would

marry Alonso de Lugo, *conquistador* of Tenerife and La Palma, and continue her eventful life through a fierce series of lawsuits in which she
struggled to the end of her days to protect her children's rights in the
lordship of Gomera against the assaults of rival claimants and a jealous
Crown. The fact that she was mistress of the westernmost deep-water
harbour in the known world, San Sebastián de la Gomera, cannot have
been lost on Columbus, who, as we have suggested, was already
acquainted with Canarian waters and intended to start his Atlantic
crossing there. His visits to La Gomera during his subsequent navigation gained poignancy from his known warmth of sentiment towards
the lady of that island.

For the time being, however, the Talavera commission was still
silent, and not even the lures of Beatriz Enríquez and the Bobadilla
were sufficient to keep Columbus in Castile when the wind seemed
in another quarter. Doubtful of his prospects in Spain, Columbus
renewed his correspondence with the King of Portugal, but receiving
only fair words without any material advance, he determined to look
even further afield. He now had experience of dealings with monarchs
and from the rivalry he had excited between the two Courts at which he
had supplicated, he must have learned the diplomatic value of his plans.
In 1488, he travelled to Lisbon to despatch his brother Bartolomeo,
who was still engaged in his mapmaker's trade, to propose an Atlantic
expedition to the Kings of England and France. Bartolomeo spent
three years journeying and entreating. He presented Henry VII of
England with a chart illustrating the Colombi brothers' geographic
theories, and helped to arouse an interest which culminated a few years
later in the first English navigations to the New World, and though he
was unable to draw any response from the mercurial King Charles VIII
of France, Bartolomeo at least helped along the overseas curiosity of
some of the French nobles. But these negotiations, Columbus knew,
must be slow to mature if they were ever to bear fruit at all, and the best
of his poor hopes were still in Castile when he returned there in 1489.

He trailed in undiminished optimism behind the monarchs' Court as
it travelled the battlefields of the Granadine war, tactfully relating his
pleas on behalf of his own enterprise to the context of the struggle
against Islam. It was probably at the siege of Baza, when an embassy
arrived from the Sultan of Egypt in a maximum of exotic pomp to
threaten the monarchs with retribution upon the Christians of the east
for the approaching fate of the Moors, that Columbus pledged the
profits of his enterprise to the conquest of Jerusalem and urged Isabella
to do the same. The monarchs might have recognised this as a

symptom of mental instability or at least as an overflowing of the millennial fantasies which Columbus, in the state of paranoia induced by
the frustration of his mighty ambitions, was harbouring in his breast.
Preoccupations with Jerusalem were to recur in Columbus's stormy
brain at later moments of stress. But in fact the recover of the Holy
Sepulchre was an objective to which Ferdinand and Isabella, who
styled themselves King and Queen of Jerusalem, were actively committed, even though they smiled at the naïveté of Columbus's expectations.
The mention of Jerusalem must have done his cause more good than
harm. The war with Granada continued to distract the monarchs from
his case, however, and his hopes in them were soon further impaired by
the final and unfavourable report of the Talavera commission, ten-
dered some time in 1490. Columbus was still technically the sovereigns'
pensioner, but he received letters of commendation more often than
cash and was living in extreme indigence on the meagre profits of book-
and map-selling, and on the charity of friends. He might have forsaken
Spain altogether, pinning his prospects on Bartolomeo's supplications
elsewhere, and was certainly considering fleeing to France, but two
factors revited his failing hopes: the favour of the Queen, and the
growth of the party of his supporters at Court, as the result of his unflag-
ging self-recommendation throughout the disappointments of the
previous six years.

His partisans now included Diego Deza, the great theologian and
tutor of the heir to the crown, Prince John. The monarchs clearly
valued the opinion of this future Grand Inquisitor and Primate of
Spain. Deza's favour of Columbus was greatly fortified by that of the
then primate, Pedro de Mendoza. There was also a group that was to
emerge as a source of finance for Columbus's plans that at the last made
all the difference to the success of his suit – for lack of funds was the
most serious obstacle to any undertaking by the Spanish Crown in this
period: these included Luis de Santángel, treasurer of the Crown of
Aragon, and Gabriel Sánchez, his colleague, probably with the wealthy
Sevillan Genoese Francesco Rivarolo, who was not resident at Court
but had influence there; it should be remembered that Columbus
already had Alonso de Quintanilla de Francesco Pinelo on his side. He
won the confidence too, perhaps through the offices of Beatriz de
Bobadilla, of her influential cousin the Marchioness of Moya, who had
been Isabella's childhood confidante and with her husband, Andrés de
Cabrera, continued high in the Queen's favour. Lastly, Columbus had
the support of Fray Antonio de Marchena, the only Court astronomer
to credit Columbus's geographical speculations. Columbus later paid

tribute to the singularity of Marchena's help when he reflected, writing from the New World to the monarchs some eight years later: 'Your Highnesses already know how I wandered for seven years in their Court, entreating them to this design ... and never in all that time was there a pilot or mariner or philosopher or other expert but said my proposal was false, and that I had help from none save Fray Antonio de Marchena.' Marchena maintained his confidence in Columbus, since in 1493 the monarchs suggested they go in one another's company on Columbus's second Atlantic voyage 'for he is a good astronomer, and it always seems to us that he agreed with your opinion'.

Fray Antonio pursued astronomy as a pastime from his duties as head of the Franciscan province of Andalusia. It may have been through his offices that Columbus obtained an introduction to the last link in the circle of influence that was eventually to prevail on Ferdinand and Isabella to endorse the Atlantic plan. Queen Isabella's confessors were always men who commanded her obedience in spiritual matters and her respect in temporal, and it was for her confidence in their counsel that she chose them. Hernando de Talavera, for instance, owed much of his influence to his confessorial job. Another royal confessor was an associate of Marchena's who lived as warden in the Franciscan house of La Rábida, by the seamen's hamlet of Palos, which overlooked the Atlantic from its position at the mouth of the greatest river of southern Spain, the Guadalquivir. It was probably not by accident that Columbus called at La Rábida one midsummer day in 1491 and sought an interview with Fray Juan Pérez. The legend that makes him call at the monastery for the first time six years earlier, begging sustenance in his poverty for his fainting son, mixes the confused testimony of forgetful witnesses with the smack of romance. The reception he got from Fray Juan justified the permanent place won thenceforth by La Rábida in Columbus's heart. After consultations with a local astronomer, Dr Gregorio Fernández, and the shipowner who was later to assist materially and in person with the great voyage of discovery, Martin Alonso Pinzón, the warden departed for Court to seek a new audience for Columbus. He successfully persuaded the Queen, who sent money to clothe Columbus and relieve him in his distress, together with permission to hire a mule to ride to her presence – a great privilege, conceded only because Columbus's straitened circumstances had injured his health, for the monarchs were at that time fostering equestrianism in Castile as part of their war effort and had restricted the use of mules accordingly.

The involvement of Martin Pinzón suggests that Columbus's

shipping was now arranged – though not, as yet, the necessary finance. Perhaps the need for a new audience suggests that his plans were fuller than previously. When he arrived before Ferdinand and Isabella at the camp of Santa Fe by the walls of Granada, they had assembled a new and more specialised collection of experts to hear his views. It may have been now that Columbus chose to reveal the route by which he meant to sail, which was not mentioned in any surviving account of his negotiations with his patrons, but which definitely involved a passage to the Canary Islands and from there a straight westing into the unknown. He may have favoured departure from the Canaries because of a belief among some scholars that Cipangu lay on their latitude – but there was no real basis in Marco Polo for assessing the whereabouts of that island, save that it was an inaccurate fifteen hundred miles out from China. Or he may have been influenced by the widespread theory that the richest products came from southerly latitudes, without wishing to prolong his voyage by striking too far south. He may have had in mind the fact that by treaty with Portugal, the Canaries were the only zone in which Castile was permitted to expand. He must have been attracted by the harbour of San Sebastián de la Gomera, whose suitability for his purposes we have already remarked. But the most convincing explanation of his journey is that he already knew those waters and intended to exploit the prevailing easterlies. Had he enjoyed even more experience of the region, he might have ventured a little further south into the direct path of the trades, but he must have known enough to make use, if not full use, of the winds of the area. It is unlikely that Columbus can have chosen such a favourable route by chance. Certainly, it was the following wind that took his vessels to the New World, whereas previous forays into the Atlantic had been driven back by the westerlies on their more northerly tracks. Considered from another point of view, the historical accident that gave Spain the Canaries while reserving the Azores for Portugal, ensured that it was the former nation and not the latter that discovered America.

Despite the new and promising route Columbus had devised for his voyage, the only expert to approve his scheme was still Fray Antonio de Marchena. Columbus had made enemies as well as friends at Court by his ambition and vanity. He was suspected as a foreigner, detested as an upstart. 'The derisive Italian', they called him: above all, it was the titles and honours he entreated for himself that started the fires of his detractors' hatred. These were days pregnant with promise for the future, with the Court encamped expectantly about the walls of Granada, anticipation rife of the coming expulsion of the Jews, and expectation general that a new and glorious era was about to dawn. But the one man excluded from the atmosphere of hope, save by his own indomitable temperament, was Christopher Columbus. On the second day of the new year, 1492, Ferdinand and Isabella rode into Granada as conquerors. Within a few days, Columbus turned his back on the triumph and rejoicing and rode disconsolately towards La Rábida in the belief that his suit had failed.

The change in his fate could not have occurred more dramatically than when, after a day on the road, he was overtaken by a royal messenger who demanded his immediate return to the monarchs' camp. It was probably the exigencies of royal finance, rather than the unfavourable chorus of expert opinions, that had forestalled Columbus. Yet even while the explorer's fortunes were struggling through their most malignant phase, Luis de Santángel had been busy raising funds whereby the enterprise could be advanced without embarrassment to the royal finances. He obtained some support from the Genoese of Seville and more, no doubt, from Francesco Pinelo and other sources at Court, and made up the rest from his own speculations with his receipts as royal treasurer. The fall of Granada must also have allowed Ferdinand and Isabella to broaden the scope of their undertakings. The Queen gratefully accepted the chance to favour an adventurer whom she had liked from the first, and realise an enterprise which had always attracted her, or as Columbus himself later put it, 'Everyone else was disbelieving, but to the Queen, my Lady, God gave the spirit of understanding ... and great strength, and made her heiress of all, like a very dear and well-loved daughter.' Columbus made the first leg of his Atlantic voyage by mule to the camp of Santa Fe.

After so many disappointments, the success of his quest for patronage seemed like a miracle. With his strong sense of providence, Columbus believed that his opportunity had been created by God.

3

The Success of an Illusion

Indians making wine: a woodcut from Benzoni's
Historia del Mondo Nuovo (1563).

ABOUT SEVENTEEN YEARS LATER, when Columbus had made his final voyage over the sea of death, a young Spaniard, noble by both nature and blood, who had settled successfully in the New World discovered by Columbus, sat listening to the heated preaching of the Dominicans in the capital city Columbus had founded there. Bartolomé de Las Casas – for that was his name – experienced a sudden revelation. He found himself sharing the friars' outrage at the corrupt lives of the colonists and their ruthless exploitation of the wretched natives. He felt convinced that God had ordained the discovery only so that the Indians should be able to hear His word preached. It was, he thought, part of an accelerated process of Divine relation that would herald the end of the world. Las Casas selflessly devoted the rest of his sensitive and industrious life to his conviction, becoming a preacher himself and later a bishop, organising the evangelisation of unvisited areas and struggling to liberate and hallow the lives of the Indians already under Spanish rule. Greatest of all the many books he wrote in pursuit of his aims was a *History of the Indies*, which he compiled – it is true – *à parti pris*, but with laborious fidelity to the sources. Evidently, Columbus had for Las Casas a special place in the sacred story as the instrument whereby the divulgation of the gospel was made possible in the New World. Columbus's own sense that he was the executor of a divine mission appealed to Las Casas and won his sympathy. The Dominican neophyte therefore assiduously read, marked and in most cases copied as much of the discoverer's writings as he could find. Above all, the copious relations of his voyages which Columbus used to make for the information of his royal sponsors now survive only in the summaries, transcripts and paraphrases made by Bartolomé de Las Casas. To his piety we owe most of what we know of Columbus's navigations.

Not ten months after Columbus had looked gratefully up at Queen Isabella in Santa Fe, Captain Cristobal Colón – for the Portuguese form of his name had been thus Castilianised – leaned on the brine-scrubbed prow of his flagship, *Santa María*, with a similar expression on his face, only more intense now and wearier, and thanked God for sight of land at the end of his Atlantic passage. It had been a remarkably rapid voyage, with favourable winds almost all the way – but as it was the first of its kind, the mariners had no yardstick by which to measure their luck, so that to them the thirty-seven days they had spent at sea appeared interminable. And their way seemed prolonged by their uncertainty of how far they had to go and by the numerous false land-falls that alternately raised and dashed their hopes. Columbus must

Bartolomé de Las Casas:
an illustration from the biography of Columbus by J. B. Thatcher.

have had many opportunities during the crossing to reflect on the tough negotiations with the monarchs and months of preparations that had preceded the voyage.

The spring of 1492 was taken up with bargaining over the remunerations and privileges he was to receive in the event of success. Columbus immediately arrogated to himself the elevated style of 'Don', but the monarchs intended that his aspirations to nobility should be satisfied only if his voyage proved profitable. His other requests, again contingent on success, were for the office of Admiral, with jurisdiction over the Ocean Sea on the same terms enjoyed by the hereditary admirals of Castile's home waters, the governorship of any lands he might discover and a share of the anticipated profits. The monarchs were generally unstinting in meeting his requests, for no price would be too high to pay for the benefits of new, lucrative discoveries, and Ferdinand and Isabella were confident of controlling the effects of their concessions; Columbus's 'broad power', as he called it, was expressed in the 'Capitulations' drawn up at Santa Fe, where they were broadly approved by the monarchs, and a letter of privilege of 30 April 1492, which re-cast the Capitulations in the form of a royal grant. After Columbus's return from his voyage of discovery, a royal letter of May 1493 made explicit the extension of his functions from the islands to the open sea within the limits of his admiralty, while finally in 1497 the concession of a *mayorazgo*, or right to make his whole estate hereditable by his elder son, had the effect of confirming the hereditary nature of his offices and protecting them from division or revocation.

The grants made to him were of two types – economic concessions and jurisdictional or administrative rights of a distinctly feudal character. On the economic side, Columbus was to receive one tenth of the profits of his admiralty over and above the other dues consequent upon the office of admiral – though in practice he never received all of these. Where his formal powers of feudal eminence and jurisdiction are concerned, the source of Columbus's power lay in the conjunction of the offices of Admiral, Viceroy and Governor and their being made inseparable and hereditary. The effect, one could suggest, was to turn the Ocean Sea and all its lands into a feudal seigneury only a short way removed from a principality. Columbus was to have, firstly, in his own sphere, all the jurisdictional rights of the admirals of Castile, consisting of dispensing the highest form of justice and imposing the penalty of death. He also possessed the right of pardon and could judge cases arising in Castile in connexion with the Ocean trade. The nomination of subordinate officers Columbus did not enjoy in its entirety, but could only present a short-list to the monarchs – it seems doubtful, however, whether this modification applied in practice. The organisation of fleets Columbus was to share with royal nominees, but, as events were to prove, a great degree of liberty of navigation was inevitable in the early years of the discovery. As Viceroy and Governor, Columbus would be able to enjoy similar rights of jurisdiction and appointment and could command the obedience due to the monarchs. His dignity as Viceroy, being hereditary and inseparable from his other charges, was higher than that of the Aragonese viceroys, on whose office his was modelled.

It seems that Columbus gave rather more thought to the implications of these concessions than did the monarchs; later, as the enormous extent of his discoveries was revealed, Ferdinand and Isabella were obliged to disregard or supplant many of his offices and powers. Theoretically, the only means open to them to restrain him was the judicial investigation of a governor's conduct, the *residencia* or *pesquisa*, to which he was submitted twice during his term. He was the only official of the Spanish Crown up to that time, apart from Alonso de Lugo in Tenerife, to undergo such a process while still in office. The same means were used to keep his son and successor, Diego Colón, in check. The fact that Columbus was never able to rule his domains in surly independence was partly a consequence of the fact that he exercised his privileges not in his own right but as representative of the monarchs: the local opposition that grew in the colony was able both to complain and to act. Moreover, his colony was to be so underdeveloped that Columbus had few opportunities to apply his jurisdictional powers – and he had perforce to spend much of his time in Castile. The monarchs were able to interpret the terms of their grants in a way most unfavourable to Columbus, depriving him of his privileges and breaking the exclusivity of his titles and offices. After an arduous litigation, the Columbus family finally gave up their claims to Columbus's privileges, long after their substance had been lost, in 1556. In more dramatic terms, the episode can be seen as the triumph of a centralising monarchy over a feudal tendency at the periphery of its empire.

These ramifications, however, were unforeseeable when Columbus left Court for the coast with his 'capitulations' under his belt, and weighed anchor with a prayer on his lips. He departed from the harbour of Palos, beneath the very walls of the monastery of La Rábida, on 3 August 1492. His first destination was the Canary Islands, and thereafter Cipangu, perhaps, or Mangi, the easternmost province of Cathay, or Quinsay or Zaitun, its fabled ports. Hopes of reaching China were represented by one of the most curious credentials in the captain's baggage, letters of credence addressed to the legendary ruler of these parts, the Great Khan, barbarously Latinised as '*Magnus Canus*'. Ferdinand and Isabella in these letters introduced their admiral, expressed their friendship for the Khan and said that they had heard of his admiration for and interest in their realms. In fact, no ruler of China had borne such a title as Great Khan for more than a century, and none had ever heard of the Spanish monarchs, much less admired them, but the reference recalled a tradition from the thirteenth and fourteenth centuries that the emperors of China were curious to establish diplomatic contacts with the west and learn about Christian doctrines. Columbus bore duplicate letters of credence with the names of the recipients left blank, and was accompanied by an Arabic interpreter, since it was thought that by that language or one related to it the explorers would be able to communicate with any oriental peoples they might meet.

All this paper ballast was the least important of the commodities Columbus had to prepare for the voyage. The monarchs ordered the town of Palos to provide two caravels as quittance of a fine which the municipality owed the royal treasury. The first of these was the square-rigged *Pinta*, so called after its owners, the brothers Pinzón, and the other the *Niña*, owned by Juan Niño, who was also to captain her on the ocean crossing. The *Niña* was a fast, trim vessel of moderate size, rigged with triangular sails, and the *Pinta* of about the same bulk but slightly slower. The largest ship – though not by much – was the ill-destined flagship *Santa María*, with her very round hull and ponderous gait, and the proud monograms of Ferdinand and Isabella on her mainsail. The crews were recruited mainly in Palos and Seville, probably by Martin Pinzón, who also captained the *Niña*. The task of recruitment was eased by a royal pardon extended to any condemned men who shipped on the voyage, but the men, like the ships, proved reliable and seaworthy. There were a little less than a hundred of them in all. No soldiers or settlers accompanied them, for this first voyage was consciously one of exploration.

Before departing, Columbus loaded a great store of truck to trade with, which he hoped to replace with samples of spices and gold, and, though he expected to re-victual in the Canary Islands, he took on the salt fish and bacon, biscuit and flour, wine, water and olive oil that sustained all seamen. He had all the ship's tackle he needed, but probably took few sophisticated navigational instruments, for Columbus, after the fashion of his time, navigated by a mixture of intuition and divination – a compass and an hour-glass were all that were needed. Columbus made an unfulfilled promise to the monarchs that he would keep track of his latitude and longitude during the voyage, so that he must have taken a quadrant, at least, and perhaps some works of astronomy and navigation, but on this voyage, there is no evidence that he ever used them.

The passage to the Canaries was rapid and uneventful; for the major part of the ocean crossing, Columbus had the *Niña* converted to square rigging, which would catch the following wind – another indication that he knew the sort of winds to expect. The temptation to linger in the islands must have been great in the element season, with so many unknown dangers in the offing and the chance of seeing Doña Beatriz de Bobadilla before making a final departure. But Columbus could not afford to miss the easterlies and on Thursday, 6 September 1492, they quit San Sebastián amid a flurry of square sails, and leaving the isle of Hierro to starboard, took their leave of the known world.

The crossing was dominated by three recurrent themes: the phoney landfalls, which undermined the men's morale; the fears as the wind carried them swiftly westward that they would never find a wind to take them home; and Columbus's own barely perceptible but genuine doubts, which afflicted him increasingly as his expedition spent longer and longer out of sight of land. They rapidly negotiated the dangers of a Portuguese squadron sent to intercept them and the mysteries of the Sargasso Sea, of which they certainly had preliminary notice to allay their fears without diminishing their amazement, but the insidious element of uncertainty about their destination and the advisability of their voyage made the fair passage a time of torment. Columbus's entries in his prolix journal in mid-September read like the story of Noah's Ark:

Thursday, 20 September. He set course this day west by north and at half sail because conflicting winds succeeded the calm. They would make seven or eight leagues. There came to the flagship two pelicans and later another, which was a sign of nearness to land. By hand they took in a bird which was a river-bird, not of the sea, though its feet were like a gull's. There came to the ship at dawn two or three landbirds singing and later before daybreak they departed...

Columbus soon half-revealed to himself his own doubts of the distance to the Indies, for from 19 September he began to falsify the ship's log, undercutting the number of miles they had traversed in the estimates he retailed to the men. In fact, since Columbus's approximations of distance always tended to be overestimates, the falsified log was more accurate than the private one he kept for himself. He welcomed the slightest indication as a sign of nearby land – a chance shower, a passing bird, a supposed river-crab, and on 25 September declared himself certain that his fleet was passing between islands – but he did not feel confident enough to turn and look for them, though they were marked on a speculative chart which he had with him. On 22 September the crew's anxieties were such that Columbus was glad of an opposing wind. 'I needed such a wind', he wrote, 'because the crew now believed that there were winds in those seas by which we might return to Spain.'

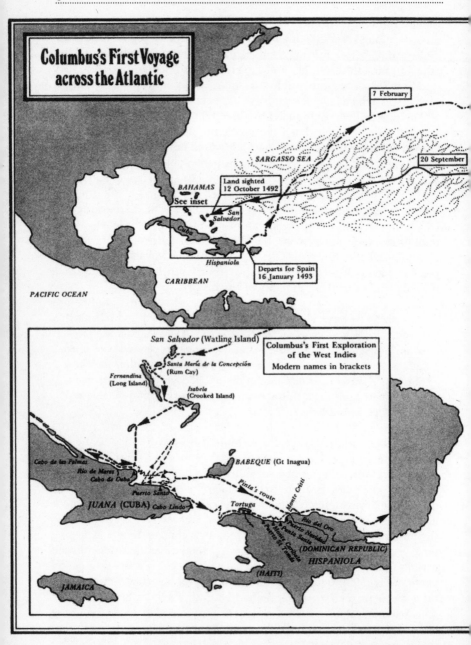

Columbus's First Voyage across the Atlantic

7 February

SARGASSO SEA

20 September

BAHAMAS
See inset

Land sighted
12 October 1492

San Salvador

Cuba

Hispaniola

Departs for Spain
16 January 1493

CARIBBEAN

PACIFIC OCEAN

San Salvador (Watling Island)

Columbus's First Exploration of the West Indies
Modern names in brackets

Santa María de la Concepción (Rum Cay)

Fernandina (Long Island)

Isabela (Crooked Island)

Cabo de las Palmas

Rio de Mares
Cabo de Cuba

BABEQUE (Gt Inagua)

Puerto Santo

Pinta's route

JUANA (CUBA) Cabo Lindo

Tortuga

Monte Cristi

Rio del Oro
Puerto Navidad
Punta Santa
Monte Caprera
Puerto S. Tomás

(DOMINICAN REPUBLIC)

HISPANIOLA

(HAITI)

JAMAICA

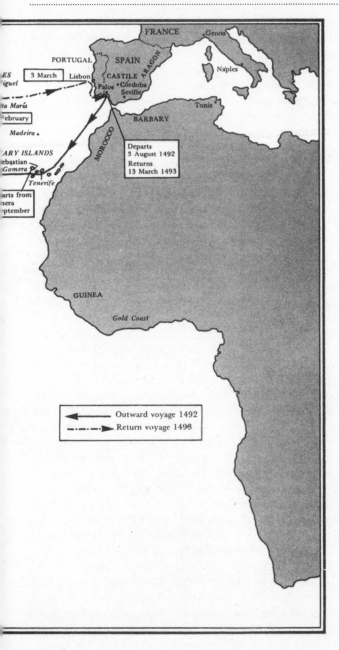

By the end of the first week in October, when patience must have been at a premium throughout the fleet, Columbus and Pinzón met for an acrimonious interview. So far they had maintained their westing into the zone where, according to Columbus's early calculations, they ought to have found land. In particular, they must have overshot or been very close to the island of Cipangu. Columbus's account of the exchange with Pinzón is obscurely expressed, but it seems that the shipowner believed that Cipangu had been missed and that they should alter course to the south-west and make for the mainland; the Captain agreed with him that if they overshot Cipangu, 'it was better to go first to the mainland and afterwards to the islands'. Elsewhere, however, he expressed a private theory that they had made less than their calculated distance owing to an imagined drift to the north. This was perhaps why he clung to the possibility that Cipangu might still lie in their path. He resolved not to alter course till all hope was gone. There was still some enthusiasm left in the fleet, the *Niña* using her speed to run ahead and try to gain the prize of royal bonds offered by the monarchs to the first man to sight land, but the uncertainty was becoming intolerable. Las Casas laconically summarised Columbus's journal for 10 October: 'At this point the crew would endure no more.'

In fact, the worst moment of the voyage passed that very day. On the 9th Columbus had abandoned the chase of Cipangu and altered course to west-south-west, and this change combined with new signs of populated land at hand on the 11th helped to calm the explorers' fears. Las Casas paraphrased the journal: 'The Admiral had it for certain that they were next to land. He said that to the first man to call that he had sighted land he would later give a bolt of silk, without counting the other rewards which the King and Queen had promised.' That night, Columbus thought he discerned a light on the horizon, which he tentatively – and certainly wrongly – took to be land. But that was the last of the false landfalls. At two o'clock on the morning of Friday the 12th, a seaman of Seville, Rodrigo de Triana, straining from aloft on the *Pinta*, set up the cry of '*Tierra, tierra!*' ('Land, land!'). The lombard shot – the agreed signal for land – rang out and was answered on all three ships with praises to God for their answered prayers.

Two things in particular struck Columbus about the island when he disembarked to examine it in the morning light and take possession of it, with royal banner streaming, for Ferdinand and Isabella. It struck him as of pleasant aspect, well watered and wooded with an abundance of fruit, and he was deeply impressed by the natives who came out wide-eyed to look over their prodigious visitors. In the first place, these

1. An impression of Columbus by an unknown artist: this portrait is now in the Uffizi, Florence.

2. The sphere on a plane surface: a diagram illustrating the construction of Ptolemy's second projection, as described in Book VII, Chapter VI of Ptolemy's *Geography*. This illustration comes from the edition of 1522 edited by Laurentius Phrisius.

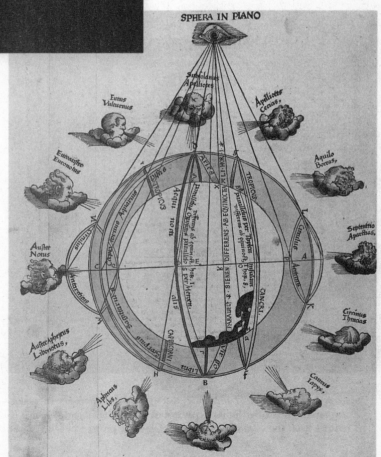

3. A map of the world according to Ptolemy, the discovery of whose writings expanded the rather limited concept of the medieval *mappa-mundi*. This map comes from the edition of Ptolemy's *Geography* printed in Ulm in 1482.

4. A map of the world by the German Hans Rust, *c.* 1480, following the conventional *mappa-mundi* style, including the 'earthly paradise' at the top. The two smaller globes show (left) the four elements and (right) the world divided into three parts.

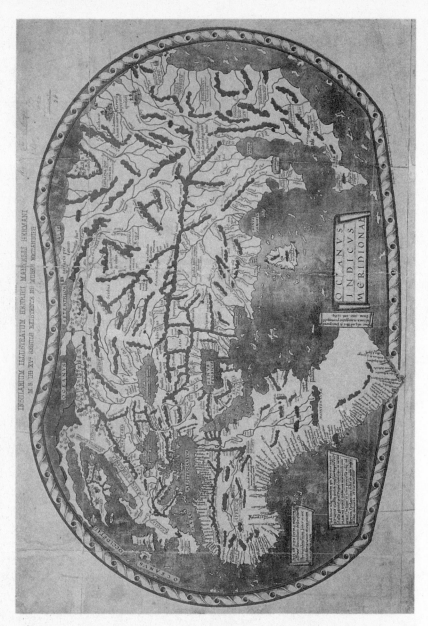

5. Henricus Martellus's map of the world, compiled in 1489. Based largely on Ptolemy's *Geography*, it also incorporates the findings of Bartholomeo Dias. The inclusion of two Asian peninsula represents one contemporary theory, which may have helped to persuade Columbus that Cuba and the Central American isthmus were Asiatic peninsulas.

6. The conquest of Granada, from the wooden bas-relief of the choir of Toledo Cathedral, carved in 1495.

7. The silver crown of Queen Isabella.

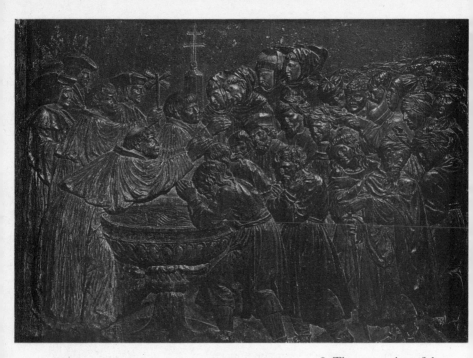

8. The conversion of the Moors under the Spanish conquest: this bas-relief from the high altar of the Chapel Royal, Granada, by Felipe Vigarny shows them being baptised.

9. A contemporary portrait of Martín Alonso Pinzón, the captain of the *Pinta* on the first voyage. Some gave credit for the success of the enterprise to him rather than to the unknown foreigner Columbus. Museo Navale, Madrid / Bridgeman Art Library, London.

10. Ferdinand II of Aragon and Isabella of Castille with Juana the Mad, from The Devotionary of Queen Juana the Mad, c. 1482. Musée Condé, Chantilly. Giraudon / Bridgeman Art Library, London.

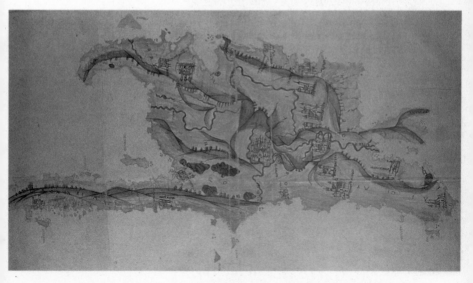

11. A map of Hispaniola, possibly by Bartolomeo Columbus.

12. Granada, a coloured engraving after Joris Hoefnagel, by Georg Braun and Frans Hogenberg from their *Civitates Orbis Terrarum* of c. 1565. Private Collection /Bridgeman Art Library, London.

people were naked. Nudity was hard to understand in the terms of a late medieval European. Clothes were the standard by which a people's level of civilisation was judged and it became an almost frantic preoccupation of the Spanish governors early in the history of the New World to persuade the natives to adopt Spanish dress, just as the Spaniards at home went to much trouble and expense to make the conquered Moors dress like Christians, or had troubled deeply over the nakedness of the aboriginal Canary Islanders. In terms of the two great traditions of thought to which Columbus and his contemporaries were heirs – those of classical antiquity and of Christianity – naked people seemed to signify an age prior to and distinct from that in which European man dwelt, either the Golden Age of sylvan simplicity, such as classical poets sang of, or the age of primitive innocence that, in Christian lore, preceded the fall of man. Judged under the signs of these paradigms, the people of Columbus's new-found island presented, because of their innocence, a unique opportunity for spreading the Gospel, and because of their primitivism, an unequalled chance to confer on them the benefits of European civilisation. Columbus made a mental note to that effect.

He was mildly surprised to find that they were not Negroes, since he was now well south of the latitude of the Canaries in zones where, according to the doctrine of the time that environment was determined

Contemporary representation of a pineapple: from Oviedo's account of the West Indies (*La hystoria general de las Indias*, 1547). Columbus and his sailors tasted it for the first time in the West Indies.

by latitude, Negro peoples might be expected to be found. But he was even more astonished to observe their docility, and willingness to please. These features were again evocative of primitive innocence, but they also pointed, even more strongly, to the prospective ease with which Columbus expected to rule the natives, change their customs to those of his own race and creed, and make amenable servants of them. He noted how pacific they seemed, and hoped – vainly as events would later prove – they they could be subjected without violence; but he misjudged them in attributing their docility to cowardice rather than innocence. From a mercantile point of view, Columbus was taken with the esteem they displayed for the valueless truck he handed them: 'I gave them things of little value', he wrote, 'and this put them so completely at our disposal that it was marvellous to behold.' He began reckoning up the chances of an advantageous cotton trade.

Columbus had therefore, on his first impressions, seen little evidence of the fabled gold and spices of Asia, but had other reasons to be satisfied. He began to think actively in terms of establishing a fixed trading colony somewhere among the islands, for he was evidently in the midst of an archipelago, and performing a signal work of piety by converting the natives; he made particular note of the apparent 'absence of any sect' among them, and thought that this would probably make evangelisation easier, a theory to which, when he later explained it to them, the Spanish monarchs also subscribed. Among all the island he would visit on this first voyage, he noted no more than a propensity on the Indians' part to lift their hands to heaven in occasional supplication to a single supreme deity, or to ascribe a measure of divinity to the Spaniards themselves. Columbus and his crew rightly acquired a local reputation as 'men from heaven'. His experiments with teaching them simple prayers and the technique of crossing oneself proved promisingly successful, for the 'Indians', as he called them, were talented imitators. And the temperance of the clime and fertility of the soil seemed to favour the settlement of Spaniards, especially as they would have such an apparently tractable labour force at their disposal.

Columbus learned that the native name for the island was Guanahani, which he changed to San Salvador (though it continues thus on Spanish maps, centuries of English rule have since imposed the name of Watling Island). In spite of the favourable indications he had found, he had no intention of pausing in his career of discovery without looking for evidence of distinctly Asiatic lands. He thought that the wounds he noticed on the bodies of the men of Guanahani and neighbouring islands might have been inflicted during *razzie* from the mainland of Asia, especially when he heard that the name of the folk responsible was something that sounded like 'Cariba' or 'Caniba', which by the rather unscientific philology he always applied in such cases, he took to be connected with 'Khan'. He was inclined to dismiss as fantastic the Indians' tales that these Caribs ate their captives, yet soon, in the explorations of the southern and western Antilles, the Spaniards would prove for themselves the existence of that ferocious race of anthropophagites from whom the name of the Caribbean Sea and the English word 'cannibal' derive. At all events, he felt confident that Asia was close at hand, and thought it worth while to enquire after Cipangu too, since the natives he encountered generally seemed to recognise gold, and some possessed trinkets of it which, they said, came from a large island not far off.

For three months, therefore, Columbus sailed about the West Indies between San Salvador and Haiti, dispensing new names to the islands and trinkets to the natives, reading references to the Great Khan or the land of Cipangu into every garbled native legend or ill-pronounced name that he heard, and always hoping that the next island in the offing might be Cipangu itself. It was in the hope of finding Cipangu that he explored generally towards the east and thereby came on the most important island he was ever to find. The native name for it was Haiti, but Columbus, having already used up the names of the members of the Spanish royal family, and most of the saints of his special devotion, on other islands, honoured the nation that had patronised his work by calling it La Española or Hispaniola, as English maps have it. Hispaniola was a significant find for two reasons: in the first place, Columbus was able to establish friendly relations – as he thought – with the natives and fix the site of his intended colony there; secondly – though it proved not to be the sought-for Cipangu – the island produced fair quantities of gold.

After coming on the island and extensively reconnoitring the northern coast, Columbus made his first contact with the local polity of Haiti near the modern Port Paix. He showed the *cacique* or chief he met there due honour and

> ... told him how he came from the monarchs of Castile, who were the greatest princes in the world. But ... the other would only believe that the Spaniards came from heaven and that the realms of Castile were in heaven ... All the islands are so utterly at your Highnesses' command that it only remains to establish a Spanish presence and order them to perform your will, for I could traverse all these islands without

The discovery of the Antilles: from an engraving included in Columbus's Letter of 1493. It shows Hispaniola and the surrounding islands which Columbus named.

encountering opposition … so that they are yours to command and make them work, sow seed and do whatever else is necessary and build a town and teach them to wear clothes and adopt our customs.

Columbus's intentions were therefore clear as he established a strong personal link, enriched with gifts and fortified by the impression made by Spanish weapons of fire and steel, with the most important *cacique*, named Guacanagari, chief of the chiefs of northern Haiti; by arrangement with Guacanagari, he took the first step towards establishing the Spanish 'presence' he had taken to heart by erecting a stockade at Puerto Navidad on the north coast and garrisoning it with thirty-nine men who were to remain collecting gold-samples and await a new expedition from Castile. He also off-loaded a good deal of his truck for sufficient gold to impress the monarchs on his home-coming, though he was unable to find any large-scale exploitable source. While he could watch the Indians pan the river for small quantities, the 'mine' he repeatedly wished for eluded him.

On balance, he was well satisfied with the discovery of Hispaniola, though apprehensive at having found no trace of China or Cipangu. He judged the island larger than Spain, and wrote glowingly to the monarchs of the virtues of its climate and the peacefulness of its people, roundly declaring it 'the best land in the world'. Events were to prove him false, but on the basis of what he had seen, it was not an unjust assessment. On a reconnaissance of Cuba, he had been disappointed to find no gold but on the basis of natives' impressive account of the extent of land that led inward from the coast, he expressed the hope that it might be continental in nature and correspond to Mangi, the easternmost land of the continent of Asia. He marked the assumption down to be verified on his next voyage. Columbus had collected many samples of gold, a little inferior 'cinnamon' – which perhaps indicated the presence of richer spiceries – rumours of pearls, and some human specimens in the form of Indians to show off back at Court. He had discovered the pineapple, tobacco – 'some leaves which must be highly esteemed among the Indians', though he did not yet know what it was for – the canoe and the hammock, which in years to come was to do much to ameliorate the sleep of his fellow-seamen. Above all, he had discovered Hispaniola, and when he set off for home, leaving only the thirty-nine men at Puerto Navidad behind, he reflected consolingly on what that island, if it was not Cipangu, might be. Perhaps he had found King Solomon's mine, or the ancient realm of the Queen of Sheba, or the country from which the Magi bore their gifts to Christ. The biblical

The fort of La Navidad under construction:
from the illustrated edition of Columbus's letter (1493).

references came to him easily then in his mood of exaltation, for another great discovery he had made was that of the people of the New World, for whose salvation, since the chance was offered him, as well as for whose exploitation, he now conceived an ardent desire; henceforth in his signature he would often expand the name Christopher into its Latin parts: *Christo ferens*, bearer for Christ, carrying His word across the Ocean Sea, as St Christopher in the fable had ferried Him over the river. He departed from his discoveries almost exactly a year after Ferdinand and Isabella had decided to send him there, on 2 January 1493. His breast billowed with more pride than his sails with wind, as, guided by his usual uncanny sagacity, he directly caught the path of the return trades that would take him to the Azores and thence back to Spain.

The return voyage was not to recapture the plain sailing of the outward trip for though the anxieties were less, the weather was worse, and after a storm scattered the fleet, the explorers' doubts about their position were almost as great. That unsatisfactory hulk the *Santa María* had been abandoned on Haiti after striking a rock, and her materials used on the fort at Navidad. It was therefore in the excellent *Niña* that Columbus weathered the tempest, while the *Pinta* under Martín Pinzón dropped beyond sight and was given up for lost. Beating her way alone through the continuing bad weather, with much of her rigging gone, the *Niña* hove to under the isle of Santa María in the Azores early on 18 February 1493. The return crossing of the Atlantic had barely been completed.

The Portuguese authorities on the island had no welcome for Columbus and his men, not because they were jealous of the extension of Castilian power which Columbus had just effected, for they probably knew nothing of it and would not have credited it had they been told, but rather because relations between Spain and Portugal were generally bad and Castilian vessels in Portuguese waters were automatically under suspicion of piracy. Ten men who went ashore to offer prayers to the local Virgin on their deliverance from the storm were clapped in irons, and Columbus had much difficulty extricating them: he still had a long run home; he had lost the *Pinta* at sea, it seemed, as well as the *Santa María* back in the Indies; and the weather was still squally and threatening. Though these hardships were small compared with the achievements he had to report and the disasters still unperceived that he would later endure, Columbus, who never suffered reverses gladly, was deeply upset; he began to take refuge in fantasy – a tendency that would become more pronounced later when his troubles grew worse. Stories of prodigies he had heard and dismissed in the Indies he now began to credit – men with tails and one eye, cannibals, the land of the Amazons, an island of bald men where there was infinite gold…

An ill wind now bore him from the Azores through more storms to Lisbon. His old friend John 11 of Portugal was not as simple as his officials on Santa María. He knew Columbus's business in the Ocean Sea and was displeased that a voyage he had refused to sponsor had turned out so well under the auspices of his rivals. It was therefore with some trepidation – but no option, in view of the state of his vessel and crew after such a taxing journey – that Columbus disembarked in the Portuguese capital. Not only was he apprehended by King John and left in doubt of his chances of release, but he also soon came under suspicion in Castile for this unexpected – though on Columbus's part quite involuntary – intercourse with the Lusitanian monarch. John, however, realised that he could gain nothing by holding Columbus in his custody and was already contemplating a diplomatic arrangement that would include concessions to Castile in the Ocean Sea in return for a safely Portuguese zone around southern Africa. Within a month of leaving Lisbon, therefore, in mid-April 1493, Don Cristobal Colón, 'Admiral of the Ocean Sea, Viceroy and Governor of the Islands he had discovered in the Indies' – as he now undoubtedly was – could dangle his gold-samples and parade his feathered 'Indians' before the admiring Court of Ferdinand and Isabella at Barcelona.

But before he did so, one more extraordinary stroke of fortune was to befall his enterprise. Miraculously, *Pinta* had been saved from the storm, though separated from *Niña*, and had struggled into the northern Spanish port of Bayona ahead of Columbus, who had been detained in the Azores and Lisbon. Martín Pinzón, we know, had disagreed at least once with Columbus during the outward voyage and the paucity of references to him in the Admiral's journal makes one suspicious that their differences had not ended there. Later, during the long lawsuit between the Crown and Columbus's family, friends of the Pinzóns constructed an elaborate legend around Martín's memory, attributing to him the major role in the great voyage of discovery. Had Martín Pinzón achieved his desire of giving the monarchs his own account of events, Columbus might have been severely embarrassed. As it happened, there was no one, save the troupe of captive Indians, to share the stage with Columbus at Barcelona; for, taxed beyond his strength by the sleepless weeks in a stormy sea, shortly after finding a haven in Castile and before he had time to tell his own story, Martín Pinzón was dead.

4

THE ILLUSION OF SUCCESS

Indians of Hispaniola washing for gold to pay the tribute
extracted from them by the Spaniards every month: an
illustration from Oviedo's history of the West Indies.

How COLUMBUS AND THE NEWS he brought were received in Europe is germane to a question we shall soon have to confront: whether or in what sense Columbus can be said to have 'discovered' America.

His own belief was that the lands he had explored were Asiatic; to himself and to the monarchs, he was sometimes able to admit other possibilities but in the face of his detractors he never wavered in his insistence that his theories about a western passage to Asia had been borne out. This was because one of the focuses of his opponents' attacks was that his discoveries had not represented the fulfilment of his promises to the monarchs: he had found a way not to Asia but either to a group of Atlantic islands similar to those already known or to an antipodal continent. Columbus's return, the letters he sent to correspondents at Court and in Córdoba, and his spectacular presentation in Barcelona, immediately aroused advocates of all three possible theories of the nature of the newly found lands.

From Columbus's point of view, it was most important that Ferdinand's and Isabella's opinion should coincide with his own. The monarchs' first reaction was to accept the authenticity of his claims, but they were not sufficiently confident of him to commit themselves irrevocably. In his summons to Court, Columbus was addressed with all the titles he had been promised upon the successful completion of his enterprise, but the lands of his recent adventures were identified only vaguely as 'islands he has discovered in the Indies'. Royal enquiries to Columbus about whether the seasons in the new lands coincided with those at home are reminiscent of some remarks of Posidonius about the Antipodes – but the matter is obscure, and other writers had connected such seasonal variations with oriental climes.

In the negotiations which were at once opened with the Pope for the confirmation of Castilian sovereignty in these areas, the monarchs' servants used even more imprecise language. If anything, the royal and papal chanceries at the time of the drafting of the Bull *Inter cetera*, published shortly after Columbus's return, inclined to the view that the explorer had found an antipodal continent, for the phrase 'mainlands and islands remote and unknown' which they applied to the discoveries appeared to exclude Asia, which was not 'unknown', in the sense used then, but merely long unvisited. The name of 'Antipodes' was actually bestowed on Columbus's islands in one of the first reports to leave Court after his arrival there, written by Pietro Martire di Anghiera (Peter Martyr), the great Italian humanist patronised by Ferdinand and Isabella, for the information of friends in Italy: 'There has returned

¶ Epistola Christofori Colom: cui etas nostra multū debet: de
Insulis Indie supra Gangem nuper inuētis. Ad quas pergren/
das octauo antea mense auspiciis τ ere inuictissimoꝝ Fernādi τ
Helisabet Hispaniaꝝ Regū missus fuerat: ad magnificum dñm
Gabrielem Sanchis eorundē serenissimoꝝ Regum Tesaurariū
missa: quā nobilis ac litteratus vir Leander de Cosco ab Hispa
no idiomate in latinum cōuertit tertio kal's Maii. M·cccc·xciii
Pontificatus Alexandri Sexti Anno primo.

Quoniam suscepte prouintie rem perfectam me ꝓsecutum
fuisse gratum tibi fore scio: has constitui exarare: que te
vniuscuiusꝗ rei in hoc nostro itinere geste inuenteꝗ ad/
moneant: Tricesimotertio die postꝗ Gadibus discessi in mare
Indicū perueni: vbi plurimas insulas innumeris habitatas ho/
minibus repperi: quarum omnium pro felicissimo Rege nostro
preconio celebrato τ vexillis extensis contradicente nemine pos/
sessionem accepi: primeꝗ earum diui Saluatoris nomen impo/
sui: cuius fretus auxilio tam ad hanc: ꝗ ad ceteras alias perue/
nimus. Eam ꝟo Indi Guanabanin vocant. Aliarū etiam vnam
quanꝗ nouo nomine nuncupaui: quippe aliā insulam Sancte
Marie Conceptionis. aliam Fernandinam. aliam Hysabellam.
aliam Joanam. τ sic de reliquis appellari iussi. Cum primum in
eam insulam quam dudum Joanam vocari dixi appulimus: iu/
xta eius littus occidentem versus aliquantulum processi: tamꝗ
eam magnam nullo reperto fine inueni: vt non insulā: sed conti
nentem Chatai prouinciam esse crediderim: nulla tñ videns op
pida municipiaue in maritimis sita confinibꝰ preter aliquos vi/
cos τ predia rustica: cum quoꝝ incolis loqui nequibam. quare si
mul ac nos videbant surripiebant fugam. Progrediebar vltra:
existimans aliquā me vrbem villasue inuenturū. Deniꝗ videns
ꝗ longe admodum progressis nihil noui emergebat: τ hmōi via
nos ad Septentrionem deferebat: ꝗ ipse fugere exoptabā: terris
etenim regnabat bruma: ad Austrumꝗ erat in voto cōtendere:

The first page of Columbus's letter to Santángel in its first Latin edition.

from the Western Antipodes one Christopher Columbus of Liguria who barely obtained three ships from my sovereigns for this voyage, because they regarded the things he said as fabulous.' To other correspondents, Peter Martyr roundly declared that Columbus's discoveries were previously unknown – by which he meant that they were not Asiatic – and though he kept the names of 'antipodes' and 'new world' or 'new orb', he was always non-committal or positively hostile whenever relaying Columbus's own opinion that he sailed to regions near India. Peter Martyr's opinion seems to have been the dominant one among the Italian humanists. In a sermon at Rome in 1497 another of them described how Columbus had taken the Name of Christ to the Antipodes 'which previously we did not even think existed', and not long afterwards the Florentine Simone del Verde designated Columbus's discovery as 'the other world opposite to our own'. This climate of opinion in Italy helps to explain how Vespucci on his first navigation to the New World shortly afterwards could refer to the lands he visited as 'antipodal regions'.

Other conflicting views were current. Immediately on Columbus's return to Portugal, it was rumoured that he had found the mythical lost land of Antilia, while one Italian observer described the find as new islands of the Canarian archipelago. This perhaps reflects Portuguese-Castilian rivalry over new Atlantic discoveries, since Antilia was by tradition a Portuguese land, while the Canaries had been guaranteed by treaty to Castile. Both rumours associated Columbus's explorations with Atlantic islands that were neither Asiatic nor antipodal in character. Despite such rumours and the views of Peter Martyr and his friends, while many scholars suspended judgment, other men were drawn to share Columbus's belief that the new lands were part of Asia: the explorer's own apparent assurance and the undoubted samples of gold he carried helped to create this impression. The Duke, formerly Count, of Medina Celi asked the monarchs of Spain for permission to exploit the good fortune of his erstwhile protégé by sending six caravels a year to the new lands, to trade for spices, in the belief that Columbus had found the spiceries near India; various Italians in Spain reported home to the same effect, but their opinion does not seem to have been as well received as Peter Martyr's: scholars generally adhered to traditional beliefs of the size of the globe and would not agree that Columbus could have sailed to Asia. Had a western route to Asia really been thought possible in Italy, where economic life depended to so great a degree on the Eastern spice trade, there would have been an unparalleled upheaval in the money market and seismic upsurge of diplomatic activity. On the other hand, in the next pontificate, that of Julius II, the papal chancery may have had an impression that the Columbine discoveries were Oriental, since a Bull of 1504 located unspecified conquests by the monarchs of Spain 'in parts of Asia', and went on to establish three new sees on the island of Hispaniola. The issue was unclear, but it is evident that on Columbus's first return, the minds of men in the Old World were rapidly able to adjust to the idea that a continent such as America existed – a new continent, different from the known land-mass, and had already anticipated its discovery under the name of the 'Antipodes'.

Without committing themselves to the view that Columbus had visited Asia, Ferdinand and Isabella were sufficiently taken with his gold-samples and his specimens and accounts of the natives to regard Columbus's discoveries as of paramount importance. The honour they showed him, as well as their eagerness to invest in further exploitation of the area, is proof of this, for they allowed him to sit in their presence – a favour no subject normally enjoyed – and ride beside them at ceremonies or in processions. They immediately embarked on two courses of action: a settlement with Portugal and the Pope, confirming their rights in the Ocean Sea, and the preparation of a new expedition of evangelisation and colonisation to be sent to the Indies as quickly as possible under Columbus's command.

The international negotiations were the most delicate part of the preparations involved in the next stage of the discovery and exploitation of the Indies. The Spaniards' aim was to agree a line of demarcation in the Ocean Sea, beyond which all new lands would be assigned to Castile. The Portuguese, departing from such a line, would take all the lands they found in their explorations eastward round Africa, until they met the Castilians, who would be navigating from the west. The effect of this, in the Spaniards' estimation, would be to assure the whole Orient for themselves, for it was not for another four years that the Portuguese mastered the difficulty of the route to Asia round the Cape of Good Hope. The so-called '*Memoria de la Mejorada*' – a memorandum on the subject addressed to Ferdinand and Isabella in 1497 and recently, though probably wrongly, attributed to Columbus, suggests that the Cape of Good Hope be treated as the complementary line of demarcation dividing Castilian from Portuguese lands in the east, and lists India, Persia, Arabia and East Africa as conquests to be adjudged to Spain. During 1493 only the question of the western boundary seems to have been raised.

While Columbus was involved in the negotiations, his own desire prevailed for a line running from north to south a hundred leagues west of the Azores, where he thought he had detected a change of clime during his voyage to a more pleasant and mellower ambiance. The Spaniards obtained papal agreement and a confirmatory Bull before Columbus's departure on his second voyage, but the Portuguese were unwilling to confine their own westward navigations within such strict limits: in the following years, their ships would push far into the Atlantic in order to get the benefit of the north-east trades in their attempted circumnavigations of Africa. The state of play on Columbus's departure in September 1493 was expressed in a communication of Isabella's to him, which also reveals the relations which persisted between Columbus and his sovereigns at the time:

Don Cristobal Colón, my Admiral of the Ocean Seas, Viceroy and Governor of the islands newly discovered in the Indies: With this messenger I send you a copy of the book which you left here, which has been so long delayed because it has been made secretly so that the Portuguese emissaries here should not know of it, nor anyone else; and for the same reason it has been done in two hands, as you will see, for the sake of speed. Certainly, according to what has been said and seen in the present negotiations here, we know increasingly from day to day the importance, greatness and substantial nature of the business, and that you have served us well therein; and we place great reliance on you and hope in God that beyond what we have promised you, which shall be most fully met and fulfilled, you will receive from us much more honour, grace and increase, as is right and as your services and merit deserve. The sea-chart which you have to make you will send me when it is finished; and to serve me you will make great speed in your departure so that, if our Lord is gracious, the chart may be commenced without delay, for you must see how important it is to the progress of the negotiations. And of all that happens at your destination you will write and always let us know; in the Portuguese negotiations nothing has been decided with the envoys who are here, although I believe their king will come to see reason in the matter. I could wish you thought otherwise, so that you would therefore not delay but proceed at once to the task in hand, to avoid any possibility of false hopes.

The progress of negotiations over the following months is shown by Isabella's next communication to Columbus on the subject, written in August 1494:

Since matters with Portugal are now agreed, ships can come and go in perfect safety ... an arrangement was made with my ambassadors and on the question of the demarcation line or boundary which has still to be made, because it seems to us a problem of great difficulty, we should like you, if possible, to play a part in the negotiations...See whether your brother or anyone else you have with you can master the question: brief them very fully orally and in writing and perhaps with a map...and send them back to us in the next fleet.

The agreement Isabella referred to was the Treaty of Tordesillas of June 1494, in which the Portuguese agreed to a demarcation line in principle and fixed the western limit at a point 370 leagues beyond the Cape Verde Islands – a decision slightly more favourable to themselves than that made by the Pope and one which eventually secured most of Brazil for Portugal. The limit which still had to be made was the eastern one. The question was never resolved. Perhaps it was only Columbus's underestimate of the size of the globe that made it seem a present problem at such an early date, for in fact the oriental limits of Spanish and Portuguese explorations were to remain separated in practice by vast distances for many years.

On 24 May 1493, Columbus was appointed jointly with Bishop Juan de Fonseca, who was later to become general overseer of the monarchs' American empire, to prepare a fleet in Seville, Cadiz and other ports to occupy the islands and mainlands of the Indies and carry on the work of exploration. The new expedition was to be much larger and grander than the first and its aims were to include colonisation as well as exploration. On his return from the first voyage, Columbus had planned what would essentially be a trading colony or 'factory' on Hispaniola, regulating the cotton and mastic trade, the exploitation of gold and the enslavement and export of idolatrous or anthropophagite Indians. On the other hand, the peaceful Taino or Arawak Indians were to be evangelised, and Columbus shipped a group of friars for this purpose: the problem of whether to enslave pacific or baptised Indians would soon be raised by Columbus in his search for economic uses for his colony. He did not intend, it seems, to settle Spaniards permanently in the Indies but to allow them to stay and apply their technical skills for short periods of a few years, gradually renewing the entire personnel of the factory. How this intention was manifested in his policies and actions as Governor of Hispaniola, and how all his endeavours as a coloniser failed, would be the dominant themes of Columbus's life and the history of the new colony for the next six years. Beyond his colonising aims, Columbus had important work of exploration to accomplish, including the reconnaissance of more islands and above all the attempt to verify his belief that Cuba was the mainland of Mangi.

The ancient and noble city of Seville: a sixteenth-century engraving. Seville became
Columbus's headquarters in Spain.

The explorations he engaged in while governing the Indies were
starred with a fate almost as evil as his colonising ventures. The outgoing voyage of twenty-nine days marked, for its ease and the expertise
with which he navigated, the loftiest point of his career but almost as
soon as he arrived in the Indies, his illusion of success began to fall
apart. He had mustered seventeen ships for the crossing, including the
trusty *Niña*, which on this occasion was to be under his own command.
He was again accompanied by Juan Niño and other personnel of the
first voyage. The cartographer Juan de la Cosa, whose name would be
attached to a famous map of the New World, also joined him, as at a
later stage did that other map-maker his brother Bartolomeo, whom
Columbus's command brought hurrying back from his adventures in
England and France. The total personnel of the expedition probably
amounted to something over thirteen hundred men. One ship was
specially designated to be dismantled on arrival to provide wood and

A galley coasting the island of Hispaniola:
an illustration from Columbus's letter to Santángel.

nails for the town Columbus was to found in honour of the Queen so
that the colony should have a capital and its political life and municipal
form familiar in Castile.

Their course to the island, again via Gomera, where Beatriz de

Bobadilla fêted them, took them slightly to the south of Columbus's track on his first voyage, so that they made their first landfall at Dominica in the lesser Antilles on 3 November 1493. This was first of a chain of new islands discovered by Columbus as he turned north and made for Hispaniola along a route which took him to Puerto Rico, or San Juan Baptista as he named it, through the heart of the cannibal country. The first major investigations ashore were made at the island of Guadalupe, so named in honour of the great Andalusian shrine and monastery which Columbus had visited shortly before his departure from Spain (French rule has rendered the island's name as Guadeloupe). The newcomers' first chance to observe at leisure the cannibals' settlements and to glean an account of their mores from their captives filled Dr Chanca, the expedition's physician, with a disgust he recorded in a letter to the municipality of Seville:

> We inquired of the women who were prisoners of the inhabitants what sort of people these islanders were and they replied, Caribs. As soon as they learned that we abhor such kind of people because of their evil practice of eating human flesh, they felt delighted ... They told us that the Carib men use them with such cruelty as would scarcely be believed; and that they eat the children which they bear them, only bringing up those whom they have by their native wives. Such of their male enemies as they can take away alive they bring here to their homes to make a feast of them and those who are killed in battle they eat up after the fighting is over. They declare that the flesh of man is so good to eat that nothing can compare with it in the world; and this is quite evident, for of the human bones we found in the houses, everything that could be gnawed had already been gnawed so that nothing remained but what was too hard to eat; in one of the houses we found a man's neck cooking in a pot ... In their wars on the inhabitants of the neighbouring islands these people capture as many of the women as they can, especially those who are young and handsome and keep them as body servants and concubines; and so great a number do they carry off that in fifty houses we entered no man was found but all were women. Of that large number of captive females more than twenty handsome women came away voluntarily with us. When the Caribs take away boys as prisoners of war they remove their organs, fatten them until they grow up and then, when they wish to make a great feast, they kill and eat them, for they say the flesh of women and youngsters is not good to eat. Three boys thus mutilated came fleeing to us when we visited the houses.

Cannibals attacking Columbus's fleet; a Venetian artist's impression (1621).

Quite apart from their bestial habits, the Caribs' warlike aptitudes and fierce courage were sources of dismay for Columbus, for he began to realise that the conquest of the regions he had discovered would not be as easy as he first anticipated. He could take comfort only in the expectation that there would be no objections in Canon Law to the enslavement of as irredeemable a people as the cannibals. Full of forebodings induced by their encounters with the Caribs, the Spaniards made their way past Puerto Rico, whose people, Chanca improbably declared, were ignorant of the art of navigation. At last, partly by Columbus's navigational genius and partly by the acumen of their Indian guides, who knew the waters from their own canoe-borne trading ventures, the fleet arrived off Hispaniola on 22 November. It was an unfamiliar portion of the south-east coast that confronted them, but they lost no time in working round to the north and the fort of Navidad, which had now been without succour, save, as Columbus hoped, from Guacanagari and the friendly natives, for more than ten months.

Within a week, the fleet was off Navidad, entertaining a party of natives sent out in canoes by Guacanagari to bid them welcome. The first intimations of disaster struck when the envoys mentioned the outbreak of hostilities on the island; Guacanagari had been wounded in battle with a rival chief, and the Christians of the garrison of Navidad had all been killed. Columbus was incredulous at the news, but it was gruesomely confirmed by the evidence which the light of the next morning revealed. Navidad had been burned to the ground, and the thirty-nine Spaniards who had remained there from Columbus's first expedition had become the first casualties of a long series of colonial wars in the New World. The local Indians' fear that they might be blamed caused them to disperse and hide, thereby only increasing the Spaniards' natural suspicions of them. Columbus alone was inclined to give them the benefit of the doubt, perhaps attributing the massacre to the work of the Caribs, or accepting Guacanagari's story of a vengeful attack by a chieftain from eastern Haiti, after the Christians had committed disorders in his land. When Guacanagari's supposed wound proved to be entirely diplomatic, a controversy broke out among the explorers. The faction that demanded vengeance was led by the missionary leader Fray Buil, whose evangelical charity was often outdone by his natural spitefulness. According to the Las Casas version of Columbus's journal,

… that Father Buil and all the rest wished to take Guacanagari prisoner but the Admiral would not do so, though it was within his power, believing that since the christians were dead the seizure of Guacanagari could neither restore them to life nor convey them to Paradise if they were not already there, and ... it seemed to him that the chieftain must be similar to kings among the Christians who have other monarchs related to them, whom such a seizure would offend.

This extract shows that Columbus has a curiously enlightened view towards the Indian chiefs, which in general would be maintained by both him and other servants of the Spanish Crown, though Indians at a lower social level would never receive the same consideration. It also shows how he had been forced to abandon his original impression of the people of Hispaniola as docile and easily subjected: on the contrary, he was now positively afraid of a native alliance against himself, having seen the destruction wrought in the camp of Navidad. It soon became clear that the massacred Spaniards had been pursued not only by the natives but by their own sins, by anticipating many future colonists with their excesses. The Indians complained that the garrison quarrelled within itself and its men had gone on a career of woman-snatching and gold-stealing about the island. It would not be long before Columbus was trying to restrain the men of the new expedition from those same depredations. What was perhaps worse, the seeds of the crime the monarchs of Spain hated most, the crime of heresy, had been sewn on Hispaniola even before the true faith could be preached in earnest, for one of the garrison of Navidad had taught Guacanagari 'certain things injurious and derogatory to our Holy Religion'. Columbus had to 'correct him therein and made him carry a silver image of our Lady about his neck'. In relating such details to Ferdinand and Isabella, Columbus clearly hoped to soften the blow that must fall with news of the massacre and to distract his sponsors from the failure of his own predictions of Indian passivity.

Columbus calmed Guacanagari's apprehensions and restored good relations between the Spaniards and the locals by presenting him with a large gift of glass beads, knives, scissors, tin bells, pins and needles and spurs, worth in all four or five *reales*, 'and therewith Guacanagari believed that he had become very rich'. The task in hand was to choose a site for a permanent township and reconnoitre the country inland, punishing the natives responsible for the Navidad massacre at the same time. Already disappointed in his expectations of the natives, Columbus was becoming rapidly disillusioned with the climate and the modalities of the land; his men suffered from the unfamiliar environment and diet, and the livestock he had brought from Spain to

El Almᵗᵉ ſe deſpide delRey Guacanagari
Edifuada la Torre de Nabidad

Vuelbe el Almᵗᵉ yalla quemada la Torre de
Nabidad ỹ los Caſtellanos muertos.

The *cacique* Caonabo and his men destroy the fort of La Navidad and massacre its
garrison: the engraving is from the *Historia general* of Antonio Herrera y Tordesillas
(1549–1625).

provision the new colony showed little adaptability. In selecting a location for the settlement, he fell between the pressing demands of speed on the one hand and a salubrious position on the other. He fixed on a foul and ill-watered spot simply because it was to hand. On 2 January 1494, just two years after the commencement of his enterprise in Santa Fe, the town of Isabela was founded in a solemn ceremony, the first, and worst-fated, township in the new world.

In reconnoitring and garrisoning the island, Columbus relied heavily on two of his subordinates, Alonso de Hojeda, the future companion of Vespucci, and Pedro Margarit. They lacked Columbus's cordial enthusiasm for the Indies, and were unmotivated by scientific or evangelical ideals. Like most of their comrades, they were interested in gain, and had come to Hispaniola for the sake of its gold, not its people or land. Columbus established Margarit in a riverside fortress inland with the aim of recruiting the Indians to work the riverbed for gold, while allowing Hojeda to roam the island in search of mineral wealth and the culprits of the Navidad massacre. Their maltreatment of the natives culminated in the execution of a local chieftain for a theft committed by members of his community – a judicial murder at which Columbus himself connived, partly from a false sense of justice, partly from the pressure of his subordinates and partly from his own uncertainty of how to treat the Indians. They had shown themselves a potential threat, had not responded as hoped to evangelisation and were proving an inefficient labour force. In the circumstances, Columbus may have been moved to make an example of some of them. It was an example which tended to increase their belligerence, though the malleable Guacanagari remained faithful, the chieftain responsible for the Navidad disaster, Caonabo, was in the full cry of 'rebellion', as the Spaniards termed it and had so far been impossible to apprehend. Spaniards, when not enjoying the safety of numbers, were in continual peril. Deportation and enslavement of the natives on a massive scale, as had been practised in the conquest of the Canary Islands, was the only remedy Columbus could think of, and in 1494 he determined to begin the shipment of Indians to the Old World. He was impassive before the inherent contradictions of his policy, for he was proposing to export the labour force on which he had planned to rely, was breaking the monarchs' precepts for the treatment of the natives and was starting a course of action which Canon Law condemned for its harmful effects on the evangelisation of primitive peoples. But political considerations within the colony and economic exigency – for Hispaniola was still bringing no profit and the amount of gold mined was minimal – compelled him to exploit the one product of the island that he had to hand for ready export. As the native problem became exacerbated, and the colonists grew rebellious under the strain of the unhealthy environment and their disappointed hopes in the easeful and auriferous qualities of the soil, Columbus was glad to leave Hispaniola on a course of resumed explorations by sea.

The progress of the colony had so far brought nothing but disillusionment for Columbus, but he still hoped to shore up one of his illusions by proving the supposed continental nature of the island of Cuba. Having left Margarit in charge of Hispaniola with a by now inapposite reminder to treat the natives humanely, he put out from Isabela with a portion of the fleet on 24 April 1494. After interrupting the exploration of the Cuban coastline to make a fruitless search for gold on Jamaica, Columbus began the quest in earnest in the last week of May. Beyond the spiritual strain imposed on him by the frustrations he had encountered on Hispaniola, the Admiral was now physically exhausted after weeks of taxing navigation amid the shoals and reefs that lie in wait for unsuspecting vessels between Jamaica and Cuba. And as the days wore on, relieved by little sleep and less evidence that they were even remotely near continental Asia, failure began to tell on Columbus's delicately balanced mind.

He took refuge in an insane insistence that he had been right all along. He snatched at any evidence, however improbable, that Cuba was part of continental Asia, inventing some of it and reading the rest into garbled associations of native words with place-names mentioned by Marco Polo. He claimed that the footmarks of large animals, including griffins, indicated the Asiatic nature of his discovery. This was not the unfounded assertion it as first appears, since large animals were indeed deemed – by Peter Martyr, for instance, and other experts – to occur only in continental lands. On the other hand, there have never been large quadrupeds on Cuba, and Columbus's visions of griffins can only have been products of his imagination, aided by the fevered ramifications of his characteristic flights into fantasy. The certainly false claim of one of his crew to have seen a man in white on the island prompted Columbus to the somewhat overstated conclusion that Cuba must be the land of Prester John, the mythical Christian prince whom some authorities located in Africa and others at the end of the Orient. And that familiar element in Columbus's syndrome, the preoccupation with Jerusalem, began to assert itself as Columbus talked to his men of leaving the islands to circumnavigate the whole world and return home to Spain via the Holy Sepulchre.

After more than three weeks of dangerous sailing along the Cuban coast, fed by frustration and fantasy, Columbus decided to abandon the exploration of Cuba. He convinced himself that he had explored 370 leagues of coast – an egregious overestimate – and calculated that no island could be so large. On that basis, he called on the ship's scrivener, who combined the functions of scribe and public notary, to record the oath of every man in the fleet that Cuba was a mainland and that no island of such magnitude had ever been known. The declaration was false on both counts, but Columbus had been taxed so much by his grim experiences that he was now beyond the influence of reason, and the men made little attempt to argue with him. They further swore that had they navigated farther they would have encountered the Chinese – obviously a rash claim to make on oath – and promised to abide by the opinion to which they had sworn on pain of a fine of ten thousand maravedis and the loss by excision of their tongues. To exact such an oath, and threaten so brutal a punishment were not the acts of a man exercising rational self-control. What is more, it seems that in his heart Columbus may have realised that he was perpetrating a lie. For the friend of his youth from Savona, Michele de Cuneo, who shipped on this expedition, was pardoned adherence to the oath, and the penalty clause shows how unsure Columbus was of the support of his men in his claims. Most of the crew probably took the oath merely to placate the Admiral, or out of fear that he might try to execute his threat of circumnavigating the globe via Jerusalem. Certainly, the cartographer Juan de la Cosa, who was among Columbus's men on this voyage, showed Cuba very clearly as an island on the world map he made in 1504.

Little solace in his distress awaited Columbus at Isabela. He arrived towards the end of June, to be greeted by his brother Bartolomeo, who had at last returned from his excursions in England and France and come to join his famous familiar. There was some comfort in seeing Bartolomeo, whom Columbus appointed *Adelantado* of the Indies, but none in the news he brought. Complaints against the beginning Columbus had made in the government of Hispaniola had already reached the monarchs' ears. In particular, Father Buil had never established good relations with the Admiral from the moment of their first disagreement over the fate of Guacanagari, and had returned to Castile to impugn Columbus. None of the colonists was satisfied with the state of affairs on Hispaniola and many had taken the opportunity to relay their complaints with the home-bound fleet that had left the previous February. Columbus's own efforts to exculpate himself had not impressed the monarchs. He was probably right to attribute the

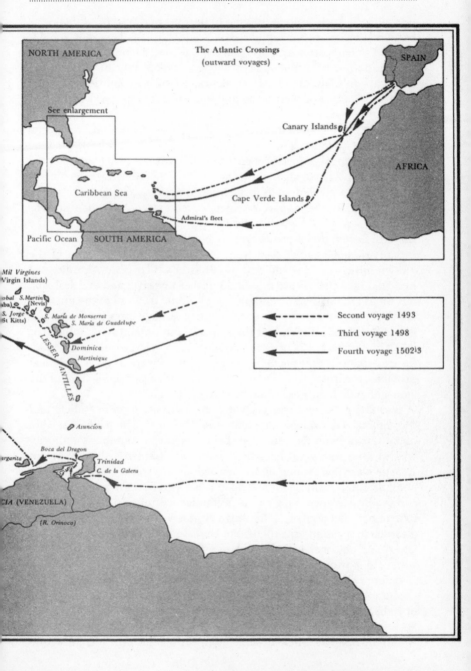

The Atlantic Crossings
(outward voyages)

NORTH AMERICA

SPAIN

See enlargement

Canary Islands

AFRICA

Caribbean Sea

Cape Verde Islands

Admiral's fleet

Pacific Ocean   SOUTH AMERICA

Mil Virgines
(Virgin Islands)

obal   S.Martin
aba)   (Nevis)
S. Jorge
(St Kitts)   S. María de Monserrat
S. María de Guadelupe

Dominica

Martinique

Asunción

Boca del Dragon

argarita   Trinidad
C. de la Galera

CIA (VENEZUELA)

(R. Orinoco)

- - - - - - Second voyage 1493
- · - · - · Third voyage 1498
——————— Fourth voyage 1502/3

prevailing sickness among his men to the 'airs and waters' of their new home rather than the syphilis which later writers have alleged. Dr Chanca's diagnosis, which also blamed the anaemic diet, lacking in red meat and wine, bore him out, but the significance of the malady was the lie it gave to Columbus's earlier assurances of the salubrious climate. This must have provoked as much displeasure at Court as dissension in the colony.

Moreover, the monarchs were offended by Columbus's plans to enslave the Indians. Their objections were partly juridical, for they doubted the legal propriety of enslaving folk who were at least potential Christians. Some of their advisers recalled the Bulls of Eugenius IV which had outlawed such behaviour. Perhaps religious objections counted too, for the monarchs may have felt that maltreatment such as Columbus proposed would interfere with their efforts to convert the Indians. Lastly, they were swayed by political considerations: while the Indians remained free, they were under the direct dominion of the Crown of Castile, according to the Bulls in which Pope Alexander VI had adjudged the sovereignty of the Indies to Ferdinand and Isabella; but should the natives be enslaved, they would pass out of the immediate lordship of the Crown into the control of their proprietors. As well as the health of his men and the status of the Indians, Columbus had fallen foul of his critics by failing to send home a large quantity of gold: his explanations that his men were too sick to work and the technical problems too great, were inconsistent with his earlier predictions of the ease with which the gold could be extracted.

Bartolomeo's news was no worse than the situation in Isabela and throughout Hispaniola on Columbus's return. The colonists were openly at war with the natives. Rebellion against Columbus's authority was brewing among the bitterly disillusioned Spaniards, the crops from Europe were performing disappointingly in the soil of the New World and provisions from Spain had been exhausted by spring of 1494. Gold extraction was dwindling to an insignificance more pallid even than that faint reflection of Columbus's bright visions which had earlier gleamed in the island riverbeds. Yet he realised that only his presence at Court and personal account of his activities could deflect the calumnies which, by Bartolomeo's account, were being sharpened by his enemies.

Before departing, Columbus took four steps which helped to create the semblance of good government in the colony. He began the export of Indian slaves – an ill-advised measure but one which circumstances appeared to urge him. He also imposed a gold tribute on the islanders whom the Spaniards held in subjection, at the same time increasing the extent and depth of Spanish rule by constructing a chain of forts. This policy doomed the natives, who had never faced laborious work or heavy taxation before, to hardship, despair and in many cases early death under the strain; but Columbus certainly underestimated the effects of the intervention of Old World life styles on New World culture, and was guilty of misjudgement rather than wickedness. His misjudgement was the worse in that the gold levy could provide at best only a short-term answer to Hispaniola's problems. The natives could hand over the trinkets they had accumulated over many years of slow extraction of impure ores from recondite sources, but until a systematic exploitation of the island's gold resources was devised, there was no prospect of maintaining the flow of gold into Spanish hands. As things were, once the Indians' longstanding stocks were exhausted, there would be nothing to replace them. And the cotton with which Columbus proposed to make up any deficit in default of gold was a substitute that could satisfy no one. In defence of this policy it must be said that it was consistent with Spanish juridical thought: for the payment of tribute was an affirmative sign of the vassaldom which, by the Pope's command, the Indians now owed the Spanish monarchs.

The remaining, more constructive measures Columbus took before leaving for Castile were to order the transfer of the seat of colonial government from the disastrous Isabela to Santo Domingo on the eastern coast of the island, a foundation which was to ensure to our own times and, one hopes, beyond, and to secure the person of the leader of the rebellious natives, Caonabo. This chieftain, the proud perpetrator of the Navidad massacre, was captured by a stratagem of Alonso de Hojeda's, who persuaded him to wear the 'bracelets' which, he claimed, the King of Spain himself wore. Caonabo condescended to don what proved to be not bracelets for his adornment but iron shackles to manacle him and keep him from further mischief.

Columbus had recovered somewhat from the misfortunes of his first two years as Governor of the Indies – at least sufficiently to hand over to Bartolomeo on his departure with hopes of greater success to come. He had addressed himself in a business-like fashion to the problems of the colony after the aberrations of his Cuban voyage. The fair crossing home in the early summer of 1496 may have helped to clear his head, beset still by thoughts of the Amazons. But the recovery of his health, as of his fortunes, was only temporary. While he accumulated instructions from Ferdinand and Isabella over the next two years for the future administration of his colony, planning his return and the renewal of his explorations amid opprobrium from his detractors, he was dangerously

unaware of the worse trials and more damaging failures that were still
to come.

5

THE INTERVENTION OF THE DEVIL

Natives of Hispaniola: an incomplete human carcass is
suspended from the beams of the hut and the natives are
making a meal out of the severed limbs. A sixteenth-century
woodcut.

THE FULL MEASURE OF COLUMBUS'S failure as a coloniser was not yet apparent when he returned to Castile in 1496. Yet by the end of seven years of his governorship, with his own and the monarchs' and the settlers' objective all still unachieved, and Hispaniola suffering an apparently interminable series of rebellions not only by the Indians but by the colonists too, Columbus would be superseded and disgraced, and shipped home to Spain in chains. He ascribed his ill success to the intervention of the Devil, but it is possible to see the operation of other factors, some of them connected with Columbus's own character and conduct.

The chief cause of disharmony on Hispaniola under his rule was the conflict of aims between Columbus and his men. Columbus felt a personal involvement with his discovery. He asked the monarchs to employ men who shared his love for his enterprise on matters connected with the life of the colony. He was resentful of anyone who did not share his faith in the merits of the new lands or who was unwilling to make as much effort as he on their behalf. Shortly after landing on Hispaniola on his return there in 1498, when he found the administration in disarray and a large part of the colony in rebellion, he began to realise that many of the Spaniards who accompanied him to the New World did not share his vision of a settler's ideal life, but were interested only in the prospects of a quick material gain for themselves. Columbus wrote to the monarchs,

> Our people here are such that there is neither good man nor bad who hasn't two or three Indians to serve him and dogs to hunt for him and, though it perhaps were better not to mention it, women so pretty that one must wonder at it; with the last of these practices I am extremely discontented, for it seems to me a disservice to God, but I can do nothing about it, nor the habit of eating meat on Saturday [*sic* for Friday] and other wicked practices that are not for good Christians. For these reasons it would be a great advantage to have some devout friars here, rather to reform the faith in us Christians than to give it to the Indians. And I shall never be able to administer just punishments, unless fifty or sixty men are sent here from Castile with each fleet, and I send there the same number from among the lazy and the insubordinate, as I do with this present fleet – such would be the greatest and best punishment and least burdensome to the conscience that I can think of.

Many of Columbus's colonists were condemned criminals, who obtained pardon by shipping voluntarily to the Indies. There was

1. An attempt is made on the lives of the Marquis and Marchioness of Cadiz – wrongly thought by the assassin to be Ferdinand and Isabella – during the siege of Málaga: from the wooden bas-relief of the choir of Toledo Cathedral, carved in 1495.

2. Indians sowing maize, from Theodore de Bry's *Americae Tertia Pars* (1591-2).

3. The Plaza del Rey, Barcelona.: here Ferdinand and Isabella received Columbus on his return from the highly successful first voyage.

4. Alejo Ferdinández's painting of *La Virgen del Buen Aire* or *The Madonna of the New Navigators*, in the Alcázar, Seville. It shows Columbus, Vespucci and one of the Pinzón brothers on the Virgin's left, and Ferdinand and Bishop Fonseca on her right.

5. Pope Alexander VI, from Pinturicchio's fresco in the Borgia apartments in the Vatican.

6. Columbus's coat of arms, from the *Book of Privileges* conferred on him by the Catholic Rulers. The first and second quarters bear versions of the emblems of Léon and Castile, below which are islands and anchors, the latter evoking the admirals of Castile. The device in the centre is the coat of arms which Columbus claimed as his own.

7. Indians present their gold tribute to avaricious Spaniards.

8. The Indians take their revenge by pouring molten gold down the throat of a Spaniard. In the background human limbs are being cooked and another victim 'carved'. Both prints are from de Bry.

9. The elaborately sculpted tomb of Columbus in Seville Cathedral, by Arturo Melida. The navigator ended his days a sick and disappointed man, clinging to his private obsessions.

10. A section of a world map of 1532, printed in Basel. This map is one of the first to show the continent of America as it would be recognised today.

11. One of Columbus's navigational aids: an astrolabe that belonged to the Viennese astronomer Georg Peuerbach, *c.* 1457. The problems of navigation were only incompletely solved at the time of Columbus's voyages. Many of the intsruments available were clumsy to use and inaccurate. John II of Portugal summoned a commission of mathematical experts in 1484 and some of their findings were published in *Regimento do astrolabio e do quadrante* (*The Regiment of the Astrolabe*), a manual for the practical guidance of sailors.

12. Vasco da Gama: a portrait by a contemporary artist.

13. A modern view of the Virgin Islands, looking Westward from the west end of the island of Tortola.

14. The urn containing the ashes of Columbus at the Palazzo Tursi, Genoa. On it is the Genoese coat of arms.

therefore a curious irony in Columbus's plan to deport them home for their delinquency on Hispaniola. In most cases, it would not have been an effective punishment, but rather the reverse, for once the colonists found how far removed from Columbus's promises were the realities of life on Hispaniola, it became their greatest wish to return to Spain, even before accumulating the wealth of which they had dreamed. Free passage to Castile was the first of the rebels' demands. In a sense, the fault was Columbus's own. He had misled his men, as he had misled the monarchs, about the nature of the newly discovered lands. The picture he had painted of large quantities of gold for the picking and willing Indians to serve, all in a salubrious climate and fertile soil, was bound to attract idlers and fly-by-nights, and above all would inevitably precipitate widespread disillusion among the men, once they discovered how hostile the environment really was, and how great the labour demanded of them. Columbus virtually admitted all this in an epistolary threnody he addressed to the monarchs in May 1499:

> None of the settlers came save in the belief that the gold and spices could be gathered in by the shovelful, and they did not reflect that, though there was gold, it would be buried in mines, and the spices would be on the treetops, and that the gold would have to be mined and the spices harvested and cured – all of which I made public when I was in Seville, because those who wished to come were so numerous. And I knew what they were after and so had this explained to them, with all the work that men who go to settle far-away lands for the first time, and they all replied that it was to do such work that they were going.

Columbus had certainly, however, stressed the ease rather than the difficulty, of peopling his new lands, if his communications to Ferdinand and Isabella are anything to judge by. It became a not unusual sight for disappointed colonists, returning from Hispaniola, to riot before the monarchs at their public audiences, denouncing Columbus and his 'lands of vanity and delusion', which they derided with surprising acuteness.

If Columbus's plans for the colony were out of step with those of his men, they did not fully coincide with the aspirations of the monarchs either. It is difficult at this remove of time to judge Columbus's intentions, but he seems to have aimed not at a settled, agricultural colony, populated by colonists at all social levels, such as existed in the Canaries, Madeira and the Azores, but at a trading colony or 'factory' of the Genoese type, or of the kind the Portuguese had established at

São Jorge da Mina on the West African coast. The settlers would supervise the introduction and cultivation of European crops and the breed-
ing of cattle, in order to furnish themselves with an acceptable diet, but
would chiefly direct their efforts towards the production of gold for
shipment home, with the cotton, mastic, brazil wood and any available
spices that would be got by truck from the natives of Hispaniola and the
neighbouring islands, and of course with the slaves. But Columbus
clearly intended that the labour resources of the colony would be supplied by the Indians. He envisaged a large floating, and only a small
permanent population of colonists, and made little effort to ship out
labourers. He selected men with technical skills – soldiers, sailors, arti-
sans, functionaries, skilled miners and agriculturists. Among the three
hundred representatives of different trades whom the monarchs
ordered him to take on his third voyage, only fifty labourers figured,
and they were accompanied by only thirty women.

Ferdinand and Isabella, however, could not be satisfied with a mere
trading factory. They wanted the new discoveries to be 'peopled' – that
is, colonised at all social levels by their own subjects, in order to bring
them firmly under the political control of Castile. As they wrote to the
municipalities of their kingdoms in commendation of Columbus's third
voyage: 'We have commanded Don Cristobal Colón to return to the
island of Hispaniola and the other islands and mainland which are in
the said Indies and supervise the preserving and peopling of them,
because thereby our Lord God is served, His Holy Faith extended and
our own realms increased.' Nothing could be more explicit.

The monarchs particularly desired that the soil of the island should
be divided among the colonists, and a new agronomy introduced, just
as was being effected by their command at the same time in the Canary
Islands. Above all they wished to promote the production of sugar, for
which there was a relatively new and quite unsatisfied demand in
Europe. They hoped by making land-grants and fiscal exemptions,
which had attracted settlers to the isles in the previous few years, to lure
colonists to Hispaniola. Lastly, the elements of the projected new
agronomy were not to be cultivated to the exclusion of the pastoral
sector, which the monarchs were determined to favour in their new, as
in their older, realms. They did not lose sight of the main purpose of all
their provision: the extension of their own power; they therefore
reserved to themselves the metal deposits and logwood of Hispaniola,
and were particularly insistent that in dividing the land, Columbus was
to alienate no jurisdiction from the Crown, but to preserve all the legal
sources of power in the monarchs' hands. These aims can be observed

in the instructions issued to Columbus before his departure on the third voyage:

> Whatever persons [the monarchs wrote] wish to go to live and dwell in said island of Hispaniola without pay can and shall go freely and shall there be frank and free and shall pay no tax whatsoever and shall have for themselves and for their own and their heirs the things [*sic* – '*cosas*' for '*casas*', houses] which they build and the lands which they work and inheritances which they plant, in the lands and places which shall be assigned them there in the said island by the persons who through you [Columbus] have and shall have charge.

The object of Columbus's permission to divide the soil was said to be the cultivation of grain, cotton, flax, vines, trees and sugar canes, and the erection of houses and sugar-mills. Now although during his years of power Columbus indeed made a large number of land-grants, the work of cultivating the crops the monarchs desired was but little advanced. Effects ensued diametrically opposed to those Ferdinand and Isabella envisaged, particularly with respect to the exploitation of the Indians.

For the monarchs and the colonists were but minor elements in the elaboration of Columbus's colonising work, compared with the problems posed by the natives. The monarchs' precepts for the treatment of this group were expressed in the first clause of their instructions to Columbus at the start of his third voyage:

> Firstly, when you are in the said Indies, God willing, you will try with all diligence to inspire and draw the natives of the said Indies to ways entirely of peace and tranquility and impress on them that they have to serve and be beneath our lordship and benign subjection, and above all that they be converted to our Holy Catholic Faith, and to them and those men who go to live in the said Indies be administered the Holy Sacraments by the clerks and friars who are or shall be there.

This expression of policy was important, not only because it restated the monarchs' avowed desire to procure the conversion of the Indians, and affirmed that they would tolerate no intermediate lordship interposed by way of slave-trading or usurped jurisdictions between themselves and their newly acquired subjects, but also because it appeared to settle a controversy which would in fact embitter the history of the New World for many years to come – that of whether the Indians were sufficiently rational beings to benefit from the sacraments of the Church. At least, royal policy on this matter was now clear. Although Columbus's requests for friars to be sent to Hispaniola usually stressed the need for the colonists, rather than the natives, to receive spiritual instruction, there is no reason to suppose that he was not as enthusiastic a devotee of the evangelisation of the Indians as his royal sponsors.

There was a political motive involved in the work of conversion: the Bull of 1496 in which Alexander VI established the juridical basis of the Spanish presence in the Indies caused Castilian rights to rest on the charge of evangelising the natives, which he laid at the Spanish monarchs' door, but Columbus, as well as his sovereigns, had already taken the task upon themselves as soon as the discovery of the Indians was made, long before the Pope assigned it to them. At the end of the 1470s, in a juridical wrangle with the papal nuncio and some unfavourable canonists' opinions, Ferdinand and Isabella had adopted the position that conversion and conquest were inseparable processes where primitive, pagan peoples were concerned. The resolution of the dispute, which arose with reference to the aboriginal Canary islanders, broadly in the monarchs' favour, had brought their political and evangelistic aims into perfect harmony. But it had not given them a free hand to dispose of the natives of the New World as they pleased. On the contrary, they were bound by a long canonical tradition, as well as their own desires, to permit nothing such as maltreatment or indiscriminate enslavement to interfere with the work of conversion, and courses which might be commercially advantageous, such as enslaving the Indians or granting them out to Spaniards as labour forces in feudal subjection, were debarred by the political necessity of preserving the Indians under the direct lordship of the Crown. In particular, it was quite clear that no natives could in law be enslaved, unless captured in the course of legitimate warfare or clearly beyond redemption because of their outrages – such as cannibalism – against natural and divine law.

It was at this point that the identity of Columbus's policies with those of the monarchs ceased. The measure of their agreement is shown by the terms in which Columbus instructed Pedro Margarit, when he left him in charge of Hispaniola during the explorations of Cuba in 1494. 'The chief thing you must do', Columbus wrote, 'is watch carefully over the Indians, and allow no ill nor harm to be done to them, nor anything taken from them against their will; but rather they should be honoured and kept in safety, so that they do not rebel.' We have already described how Columbus was obliged to depart from the lines of royal policy by enslaving and exporting peaceful natives. The only vindication he could offer was a purely commercial one. In October 1498, he informed Ferdinand and Isabella that 'as many slaves as can be sold' could be despatched from Hispaniola 'in the name of the Holy Trinity', and if, as Columbus estimated, there was a market for about four thousand of them, they would bring in twenty million maravedis 'at a modest price'. He went on, 'And although at present they die on shipment, this will not always be the case, for the Negroes and Canary Islanders reacted in the same way at first.' Somehow, Columbus's attitude to the Indians was religious without being humane. At times the merchant in him operated to the exclusion of the Christian and the visionary.

Enslavement and export accounted for only a small proportion of the natives of Hispaniola. Most of them were required to provide the labour force of the colony. Again Columbus himself expressed this best in a memorandum he addressed to Ferdinand long after he was stripped of all responsibility in the lands of his discovery: 'The Indians were and are the wealth of the island of Hispaniola because it is they who mine and make the bread and all the rest of the Christians' food, and extract gold from the mines and perform all other duties and labours of men and beasts of burden.' Once this was recognised, the problem lay in organising the Indians to the best advantage and, if possible, consistently with the monarchs' policy of benign treatment. The imposition of a gold tribute, which Columbus probably never intended as more than a temporary expedient, was clearly an inadequate answer to this need, because of the paucity of the Indians' gold supplies and the hardship they incurred. When he resumed effective government of the colony in 1498, Columbus attempted to organise some of the natives into work-parties to extract the gold under Spanish supervision, and to work the lands which he apportioned to individual colonists, under the powers conferred on him by the monarchs for the division of the soil. Partly as a result of these measures, a new polity was imposed on the New World, in which these groups of Indians became linked not to particular tasks, like gold-mining, or to pieces of land, but to individual Spaniards, who exercised over them rights which were not sovereign or seigneurial or proprietary but which were nonetheless personal. This was so thoroughly the case that the governors who followed Columbus usually bestowed not lands upon the colonists, but designated groups of Indians to serve them.

In the early years of the operation of this institution, known as the *encomienda*, the colonist concerned enjoyed the unlimited personal services of his Indians, although in law these rights were repeatedly revoked by the Crown and replaced by delegated rights in the tribute

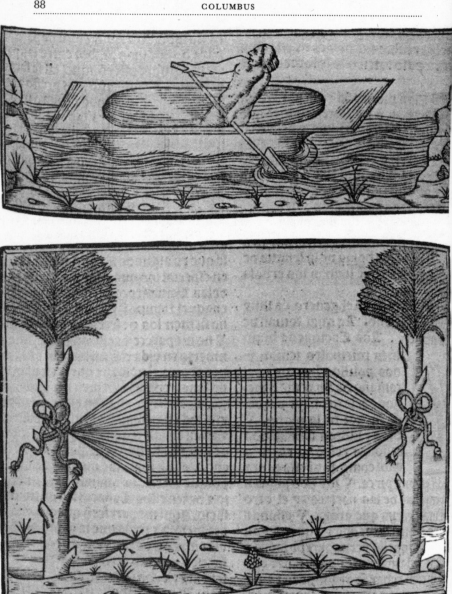

Two woodcuts of Indian life from Oviedo: An Indian paddling a dug-out canoe.
An Indian hammock.

due to the sovereign. From Columbus's day until at least the 1530s, the *encomienda* dominated Spanish society in the New World. Desire for *encomiendas* dominated men from within, its operations as an institution from without. Las Casas equated *encomienda*-lust with gold-lust: 'The gold they came to seek consisted in grants of Indians.' Most of the Indians of the conquered areas seem to have been comprehended in the system, which for a time enjoyed something of an institutional monopoly. Except for the government at Santo Domingo, the native chieftains (most of whom were anyway included in *encomiendas*) and the municipal councils, there was no other instrument of social, economic and political regulation in the conquered areas. All aspects of colonial life were embraced by it. The military institutions, such as they were, depended on it, and upon it ecclesiastical organisation, with proselytisers linked to particular *encomiendas*, was based. Commerce, mining and industry were all linked to the *encomienda* system – though less so as time went on – and the link with agriculture was even stronger.

It is therefore important to know how far historians have been right to attribute the introduction of the *encomienda* to Columbus. When the Spaniards came to the New World, nothing like the *encomienda* was known in the history of their society. Grants of land, lordship, jurisdiction and tribute all had a place in previous colonising experience, but never before had personal services been apportioned in this way. It wildly exceeds the evidence to represent the early divisions of the Indians as delegations or alienations of sovereign rights. The enslavement of the Indians could be described in those terms, for it effected a change in the status of the natives from royal vassals to personal chattels. But there is nothing in the surviving texts of early *encomienda*-grants which is incompatible with royal vassaldom, indeed there is no evidence until the coming of the Dominicans to Hispaniola that anyone thought of these grants in juridical terms at all. All the acts did was to define the Indians whose personal service the beneficiary could make use of and confer military or evangelistic obligations on him. The question of entitlement was not raised; the only hint of it was in the provision that the grantee should teach his Indians the faith, since it was on this principle, enshrined in the papal donation of 1496, that the legitimacy of the Spanish conquest was held to rest. It is true that Columbus's age was obsessed by juridical ideas but not nearly so obsessed as some later historians. One other element helped to make these grants distinctive from anything previously known: there was effectively no mention of the limits of the services involved. There were nearly always some Indians – the youngest or the oldest – who were exempted from service, and it was usually specified that the Indians were to work on 'farmlands and estates' and mines if there were any. In other words, service was to apply to all the activities for which the Spaniards required it and there were no practical limits upon it.

Where did the idea of this institution, unique in its day, originate, if it was not worked out and applied by Columbus? The records of the Admiral's administration of Hispaniola are lost, and the theory that the *encomienda* was his work rests on the assertions of historians who wrote later in the sixteenth century, above all on the testimony of the eminent antiquarian Antonio de Herrera, that 'the Admiral gave [the colonists] inheritances or farmlands whence all the *encomiendas* of the Indians originated'. The first part of this statement may be said to give the facts, the second Herrera's conclusion, but the one does not really follow from the other. Rather it seems that Columbus apportioned land, not Indians in the first instance – land which the Indians were obliged to till, the amount of land being specified and the work therefore limited. In other words, he granted land-rights with a strictly limited right of labour use – not at all the *encomienda* proper with its omission of any rights in land and of any limitation on the services of the Indians. Las Casas seems to be getting at the same point when he says that Columbus apportioned the lands of Hispaniola and allowed the Spaniards to compel the Indian chiefs to work them. Grants of this type were not inappropriate to the circumstances. Instances are recorded as late as 1508 in Hispaniola. It is worth recalling that from 1497 Columbus was expressly empowered to make land-grants. There is no evidence that he ever made grants of any other sort. On the contrary, there are strong reasons for thinking that he in no sense introduced the *encomienda*. In the first place, such an action would have no precedents, whereas land-grants were consistent with previous colonising experience. In the second, it is hard to see where the *encomienda* or anything like it can have fitted into Columbus's plans for a trading factory with an unstable population: the *encomienda* would have been inappropriate, except for a colonist who chose, as they did but very rarely, to stay and make his life in the Indies or at least remain for an extended period. Yet we have it on the authority of Columbus's companion Michele de Cuneo that most of his men intended to return to Spain at an early opportunity. Their labour needs would be best supplied by the organisation of Indians into work-bands not allotted to individual Spaniards personally, such as Columbus is known to have established for the extraction of gold.

Lastly, we have to take into account the attitude of Las Casas. Las

Casas's knowledge of the Admiral was almost unrivalled in his day. He arrived to live in Hispaniola shortly after Columbus's administration there ended and could observe the existing institutions at first hand. And he was the bitterest critic of the *encomienda* system, for he believed it was an insuperable obstacle to the evangelisation of the Indians. If Columbus had been connected with the origins of that system, it is hard to see how Las Casas could have overlooked the fact, nor knowing it have refrained from comment. Yet in his *History of the Indies*, Columbus's days appear as a Golden Age, spoiled only by the excesses of his subordinates, before the systematic exploitation of the Indians began.

In order to reconcile Las Casas with other accounts we do not have to ascribe to succeeding governors an originality we were loath to attribute to Columbus. There remains the possibility that the sort of relationships between Indians and Spaniards enshrined in the *encomienda* had already grown up casually in the days of Columbus's rule, and that the first *encomienda* grants the later governors made merely confirmed an existing situation. The example of Paraguay, if a distant but not dissimilar instance may be adduced, suggests that this is not impossible: there the Spaniards acquired personal services almost by accident – or rather the natives supplied services voluntarily when the Spaniards took their daughters as wives or concubines. There is an inconclusive but suggestive passage in Las Casas which may indicate that the situation in Paraguay was paralleled in Hispaniola:

> The three hundred Spaniards who were here [in 1502] ... used by seduction or force to take the head women of the villages or their daughters as paramours, or servants as they called them, and live with them in sin; their parents or vassals believed they had been taken as legitimate wives, and in that belief they were given to the Spaniards, who became objects of universal adoration.

It seems that here – in the casual results of fraternisation with the natives – rather than in the alleged operation of a supposed juridical idea through legislation for which there is no evidence, is where the origins of the *encomienda* lie. This conclusion is important as an example of how the institutions of the Spanish empire were moulded not as historians have claimed by 'the action of the state' but by factors in the environment of the New World. Columbus probably did not introduce the *encomienda*, but looked on impotently as the social modalities created by the Spanish presence in Hispaniola imposed that form on the land-grants he made and the native work-bands he organised.

The *encomienda* proved at best unproductive and at worst destructive. Already in Columbus's day the catastrophic depopulation of Hispaniola, caused by the spread of early death among the Indians and an unparalleled decline in the birthrate, had set in and would soon spread to other Spanish conquests. Many contemporaries felt that the *encomienda*, with its demoralising effects and burdensome – indeed, often cruel – application, was a major factor in the demographic disaster. No advantages seem to have accrued from it and the administrators of the empire devoted much of the next century to devising alternatives to it, none of which proved satisfactory either. Columbus's role in its genesis was typical of his shortcomings as a coloniser. The problems so far exceeded his capacities that he made little attempt to impose his will on events, of which he was often a passive spectator. He met his rebels, for instance, by acceding to their demands, and when he did take a positive course of action, as in opening the slave trade, it was because he admitted he could see no alternative. He pleaded to the monarchs a string of insufficiencies –of men, of materials, of personal competence.

Almost as soon as he arrived in his disrupted colony in 1498, he wrote to Ferdinand and Isabella to send him a 'lettered' official to assist in the administration of justice, since he was unable to keep the colonists in order and doubted even whether the friars whom he had asked for could do the job by admonition alone. Probably Columbus was only trying to anticipate a course of action that was already in the monarchs' minds. In other governorships and jurisdictions of their empire they were busy dismissing *conquistadores* and replacing them with University-trained administrators. They had already appointed Bishop Juan de Fonseca to administer the preparation of fleets and personnel for the Indies jointly with Columbus, and during the latter's absence in Hispaniola, Fonseca had taken sole charge of such operations in Castile. As a result, in the last year of Columbus's governorship of the Indies, began the series of so-called 'Andalusian' voyages, organised mainly from Cadiz with royal permission to extend Spanish knowledge and sovereignty beyond the lands discovered by Columbus. Among these, perhaps, Amerigo Vespucci shipped for the first time to the continent that was later to bear his name. Fonseca was intended at least in part as a counterweight against Columbus. In a scarcely veiled reference to the Bishop's activities, the Admiral asked the monarchs to appoint only those who felt affection for this enterprise, and not those who did all they could to hamper him and favour his rivals.

After receiving Columbus's requests for 'lettered' assistance, the monarchs decided to send Francisco de Bobadilla, who combined the advantages of noble birth and learned preparation, both of which Columbus lacked, with judicial powers to Hispaniola, to deal with the rebels and investigate the grievances which the colonists had accumulated against the Admiral. By the time Bobadilla arrived on Hispaniola in August 1500, Columbus was already out of patience with the 'Andalusian' voyagers, who had defiled his discoveries – as it seemed to him – by intruding upon them without his permission, alienating his natives, engaging illicitly in slaving and frequently landing on Hispaniola to foment rebellion. He later admitted that he thought at first that Bobadilla was such a one as these. He probably did not receive him with the humility and disposition to please which he claimed in his pleas to the monarchs, nor was Bobadilla, for his part, well-disposed towards Columbus. He had come from hearing the allegations of Columbus's detractors in an atmosphere at Court where foreigners, and particularly Genoese, were being made the scapegoats for the problems of Castile's other colonies. Throughout the 1490s Genoese personnel were suffering dismissal from office, losing suits at the bar of royal justice and enduring repeated legislation to limit their property holdings and sequester the surplus. When applying for 'lettered' help, Columbus had already anticipated this ground of objection to his rule. 'I have been blamed in my colonising work, as in many other matters, as a poor foreigner,' he complained, but this was not the moment to apply to the Court of Castile for that kind of redress. According to Columbus's friend the chronicler Andrés Bernáldez, the charges against him were 'that he was concealing the gold, and wished to make himself and other accomplices lords of the island, and give it away to Genoese'. Bobadilla was authorised to take the government of Hispaniola into his own hands if he found that the Admiral had a case to answer. His first acts on arrival, amid a new rebellion which Columbus was trying to suppress, were to promote the Admiral's opponents, clap Columbus and his brothers in irons and despatch them to Spain for trial of the charges made against them.

Columbus's career had now touched the depths but the circumstances were not perhaps as bad as they might at first sight appear. Imprisonment was something of an occupational hazard of high office in the Spain of Columbus's day, and though he would never again ascend to the halcyon days of 1493, some redress awaited him in Castile. He had failed in the role of oriental satrap, as he imagined himself, but – rare thing in Columbus – was willing to acknowledge the fault as at least partly his own, and blame the shortcomings of his education. 'I must be judged as a captain', he pleaded, 'of cavaliers and conquests and such and not a man of letters.' He retained his sonorous titles of Admiral, Viceroy and Governor, and the prospects of considerable wealth – even allowing for the non-fulfilment of many of the monarchs' promises – from his share of the revenues and profits of the Indies. His sons were being brought up at Court, the legitimate Diego, at least, was set to make an excellent marriage and all his family bore the noble style of Don in Castile. Columbus was unlikely to regain power in the sense of gubernatorial responsibility in Hispaniola, but though he continually sued for reparation at the monarchs' Court, the mechanics of power had never attracted him as much as glory, nobility, wealth and the excitement of discovery. As we have seen, he was eager to share the burden of rule in his colony with someone better qualified to bear it. On the other hand, his setbacks and disillusionment permanently upset his mental and spiritual equilibrium. Already on returning to Hispaniola and finding himself crossed by fate in the forms of recalcitrance and rebellion among his people, he had allowed his thoughts, manifested in his letters, to become incoherent, irrelevant and even deranged. He became self-justificatory where he had formerly been self-laudatory and found increasing relief in mysticism, millennialism and paranoic fulminations against unspecified enemies. We shall see the elaboration of all these symptoms when we examine Columbus's last years, but in the immediate term, his fettering and despatch to Castile had an effect which he sensed more acutely and resented more deeply. His work of exploration was interrupted.

The intervention of the Devil in the progress of his career occurred at a moment when he had carried his explorations to a crucial point, for on the outgoing stage of his third voyage he had become the first European since the random navigations of the Vikings to see the continent of America, and first to perceive its continental nature. In the wake of the discovery, he had undergone the most intense self-examination he ever engaged in, and given fuller expression than ever before to his doubts of his own geographic theories. First the problems of the colony on Hispaniola and then the arrival of Bobadilla had prevented him from exploring further and putting his new and his old speculations together to the test. Now he was removed from the Indies and returning perforce to Castile, while ideas to which he had held so tenaciously for so long were plunged anew into the crucible of his unreliable brain. To understand the process, and how he returned obstinately, perhaps inevitably, to the conclusion that he had been right all along, we must leave the story of Columbus's failure as a coloniser and return to his progress as an explorer, and in particular to the events of the voyage that took him for the third time to Hispaniola in the summer of 1498.

An illustration of an iguana from Oviedo's history.

6

THE TRIUMPH OF OBSESSION

Stradanus's impression of Columbus on board ship: an early
sixteenth-century engraving.

ALTHOUGH HIS INSTRUCTIONS related mainly to problems of colonisation, Columbus started his third voyage with a great deal of exploring in mind. With the gold of Hispaniola still in short supply, he remained anxious to discover a really impressive new source of wealth, and he had not yet found convincing evidence of the true nature of his discoveries, especially of their exact relationship to the known lands of Asia.

He expected to improve his chances of finding precious commodities by taking a more southerly course than on his previous voyages. The opinion was widely cultivated in his day that lands on the same latitude had similar products. It was also held that these latitudinal zones grew richer the farther south one went. Columbus therefore decided to drop to the parallel of Sierra Leone, where the Portuguese had indeed discovered gold in the lands of the Negroes, and to make his westing from there. He had it on expert advice that 'where he found Negroes, there also would he find precious things'. The good relations subsisting then between Castile and Portugal enabled him for the first time to frequent in safety latitudes where the Portuguese held sway.

There was certainly a further consideration which influenced him to seize this opportunity. According to his own record of the voyage, he was concerned to test a theory he attributed to King John of Portugal that an unknown continent existed 'in the south'. No more detailed information about the opinion of the Portuguese monarch exists than what Columbus gives us, and it is uncertain what the sources or exact nature of the idea were, or even precisely where this land was to be located. It may have been an echo of Macrobius's rumoured southern continent, or a re-interpretation of the legend of Antilia, or a theory, such as Peter Martyr and his friends espoused, of the nature of the discoveries Columbus had already made. It may have been connected with the rumours, known also to Columbus, that a new island had been sighted west of the Cape Verde group. Or perhaps it was a deliberate fiction, strewn in the wind like a siren's call by the wily King John, to lure Columbus off course. What is certain is that it raised in Columbus's mind the suggestion that an unknown continent might lie on his course along the middle latitudes of the Atlantic. Throughout the third voyage it contributed to a chronic scruple that his own discoveries might not be Asiatic in character but antipodal or 'unknown'. His references to King John's theory are important for they prove that Columbus anticipated the discovery of just such a new continent as America turned out to be.

His mood at the start of the voyage is captured in the instructions he wrote to the captains of the supply fleet which he sent ahead to

A woodcut illustrating the type of ship in which the Spaniards sailed to Mexico in 1519.
From Bernhard von Breydenbach's *Peregrinationes in Terram Sanctam*.

Hispaniola by his familiar route on the path of the trades: 'May our Lord guide me and lead me to something that may be of service to Him and to the King and Queen, our sovereigns, and to the honour of Christendom, for I believe that this way has never been travelled before by anyone and that this sea is utterly unknown.'

The choice of a southerly course made Columbus's crossing on this voyage the most uncomfortable he had yet experienced, for he sailed into the Doldrums – the windless, marine no-man's land between the zones of the north-east and south-east trades – to find himself becalmed in mid-July under a sun more savagely intense that even those torrid regions are accustomed to endure. The heat turned the ship's wine to vinegar, the water to vapour and the wheat to ashes; the bacon roasted and putrefied. The men would have been reduced to a sorrier state than the stores if the days of calm had not been mostly overcast. But a lucky south-easterly, unwonted in that season, rescued the fleet from its mephitic ordeal and bore it towards the west. By the end of the month Columbus suspected that he was approaching the meridian of Hispaniola but he had not yet had any indications of new land. He was well beyond the demarcation line that separated the zones of Castilian and Portuguese expansion, and was at least satisfied that there was nothing on the parallel he had sailed that lay on the Portuguese side. He decided while the wind was still favourable to victual and take on water in the Lesser Antilles, which he had visited on his previous voyage and which he accurately estimated to lie north of his position. When he changed course to the northward, he was unaware that the continent of America lay but a short sail to the west, at the point just south of the Orinoco delta, where the cost of modern Venezuela turns south towards Brazil.

As it happened, fate did not cheat him of his most spectacular discovery so far, for he made the mainland of the New World a few days later, but his change of course dismissed from his mind the expectation of a new continent, which had been preying on his brain since the start of his voyage, and turned him to thoughts of the islands he anticipated on his new track. Thus when he stumbled on America, his confusion about its nature – whether insular or continental – was correspondingly greater.

Columbus, when starting on a voyage, always invoked the name of God or Jesus Christ. On this journey, however, because it was his third, he dedicated the enterprise in hand specifically to the Holy Trinity. From henceforth, his devotion to that Divine Mystery was particularly fervent. When, on the last day of July, he sighted land for the first time on this crossing, in the form of three low but distinct hills just visible to the north-west, he was deeply moved by the mystical significance of the numerical coincidence. In acknowledgement thereof he named his find in Spanish the island of Trinidad, the name it still bears. Over the next few days, Columbus explored the coast of Trinidad in search of water, often in sight of the American continent, which at first he mistook for more islands.

As he traversed the mouths of the Orinoco and reconnoitred the coastline of the Paria peninsula, the intimations of a mainland at hand grew stronger. He had not altogether forgotten the prospect of finding a southern continent which had so recently been prominent in his mind, and was reflecting on his detractors' charges that his discoveries were not Asiatic but antipodal. He seems to have sought for a time to reconcile these conflicting views. On the outward stage of the third voyage he indulged in a speculation reminiscent of d'Ailly's suggestion that antipodal men might dwell in the remotest part of the Eurasian land-mass, or as Columbus put it, speaking of his own discoveries, 'These lands are another world which the Romans and Alexander and the Greeks laboured with great efforts to take' – that is, antipodal and Asiatic at the same time. It was probably this cloud-born prodigium that was in his mind when he confided to his journal off the Venezuelan coast, 'Your Highnesses will gain these lands, which are another world.' But now the terrain of the Orinoco delta acted on his brain like a catalyst to separate the two elements of this idea, for if his latest discovery was continental rather than insular, it was apparently too southerly to constitute part of the continent of Asia. Though to his own mind he might well have been close to Asia on his previous voyages, Columbus realised that any continent to the south of his earlier discoveries was unlikely to form part of the land-mass of the known world – that is, it would more probably be antipodal, but not Asiatic. These reflections were drawing him close to a true understanding of the nature of America, when decisive evidence that he was on the coast of a continent presented itself to Columbus.

The mighty Orinoco flows to the sea through four distributaries at the southern end of the Gulf of Paria, where the tenth parallel intersects the American coast. As a result, the volume of fresh water is such that no navigator can fail to be impressed. Equally, the fresh water is evidence of the proximity of a large river and so of a large body of land for it to flow through. Columbus had found little evidence suggestive of the Orient among the natives of Trinidad and Paria, though they did seem slightly more civilised – their commercial sense was more acute, the

political organisation more formal and their technology less rudimen-
tary – than the inhabitants of the Antilles. The conclusion seemed clear,
but Columbus hesitated to draw it. He was careful first to establish the
continuity by land of the Paria peninsula with the lands of the river
mouths. At last, on 14 August 1498, he entered in his journal one of the
most momentous statements in the history of exploration: 'I believe that
this is a very large continent which until now has remained unknown.'

Within a few days of finding the mainland of America, Columbus
therefore had correctly assessed its nature. Though he certainly underestimated its distance from Asia, he unequivocally expressed the distinction between Asia and the land he had found. He had described the
discovery as a new continent separate from the Eurasian land-mass. He
had not of course proved this speculation – such proof was not available
until the discovery of the Behring strait 250 years later, nor would he
hold to it consistently during the rest of his life. But he had rested his
credentials as the discoverer of America on a firm basis: not only had he
been the first to find that continent in the course of a conscious labour
of exploration, but he had also appreciated and articulated his achievement. It is a mistake to think of Columbus's discovery as a fortuitous
event, or to give the credit for first understanding its nature to any later
explorer. Columbus had in a sense been beaten to the correct conclusion about his discoveries by scholars like Peter Martyr, but by finding
the mainland and producing evidence that the New World was a continent, Columbus had turned these speculations into an empirically
based probability. This opinion of Columbus's, though he later modi-
fied it to stress the proximity or contiguity of his lands with mainland
Asia, was known in his time and quoted by his early biographers.
Although over the next ten years Vespucci, Waldesmüller, the Lyons
Academicians and others adopted it or arrived at it to some extent independently, and helped make it known and generally accepted,
Columbus was in an important sense its originator. We shall return to
Columbus's and his rivals' claims to the discovery of America before
our tale is told.

Columbus could not delay his return to Hispaniola any longer, but
he seems to have intended to carry further the exploration of the continent he had just discovered. It was perhaps the harshest change of
fortune in his life that prevented him from doing so, first by detaining
him on Hispaniola amid the cataclysmic difficulties of the colony and
then by shackling him at the hands of Francisco de Bobadilla and
returning him in disgrace to Spain. The frustration of his hopes had its
accustomed effect on his mental state. On Hispaniola he revolved all

the data he had assembled about the discoveries of his third voyage in a mind that was distracted by other problems and in no condition to process information rationally. He remembered, first, the change in the clime which he had observed on this as on previous voyages about a hundred leagues west of the meridian of the Azores. He recalled the sweet water and temperate air of the Gulf of Paria, and the fact that its river-mouths were four in number.

Lastly he adduced his astronomical observations. Columbus had worked hard to develop his stargazing talents since that first voyage, when he had failed in his promise to take readings and measure latitudes. On this third transatlantic excursion he had taken numerous readings of the position of the Pole Star, and had in fact discovered its tendency to deviate from the fixed position which most men had previously assigned to it. Columbus had first noted the phenomenon as early as his first transatlantic voyage, when his ships' compasses seemed to vary increasingly as he travelled west. He was almost at once disposed to attribute the motion to the star rather than to the fallibility of his instruments. Now he actually believed that he could measure the revolution Polaris described in the heavens, though in this he was characteristically optimistic. The movement – or at least the displacement from true north – of the *Stella Maris* had been mooted at isolated intervals in previous history, but following Columbus's re-discovery gradually became generally accepted. His deduction has assured him an important place in the history of astronomy as well as exploration, but it was based on the uncertain platform of his own inexpert observations. Rather than suppose it was his own sightings or instruments that were at fault, he assumed that the star on which he had fixed had moved. This tendency to ignore the element of error in his readings led him to a less felicitous conclusion when, in the vicinity of the Gulf of Paria, he took measurements of the declination of the Pole Star and found that it seemed to vary even more than his late discovery of its deviation could explain. In Columbus's own words,

> I now observed so much variation, that I began to wonder about its geographical implications; and I concluded that the world was not round, as men describe it, but of the shape of a pear, which was round except for the part towards the stalk, where there was bulge, or as if you had a round ball which at one place on its surface was shaped like woman's breast, and that this stalk-like part was the highest and nearest to heaven, located near the equinoctial line in the Ocean Sea at the end of the Orient.

Columbus believed that the explanation of the variation of the star was that he had been sailing uphill, so to speak, as he approached the Gulf of Paria. That would not in itself have been an improbable conclusion, were the accuracy of his astral readings not so unreliable. But the location and amenability of the place he had discovered, with the fact that it contained four rivers, tempted Columbus to a far more egregious speculation:

> I believe that if I were to sail beyond the equinox, I should find increasingly greater temperance in the climate and variation in the stars – though I do not suppose that it is possible to navigate there – where the world reaches its highest point – nor for any man to approach, for I believe that there the Earthly Paradise is located, where no man may go, save by the grace of God.

Columbus had now gone quite beyond the evidence. To the world's putative breast he had added an imaginary nipple and placed the Garden of Eden on its top. With the recollection that many scholars believed Eden to lie at the end of the Orient, he had confused his own obsession with the supposed Asiatic nature of his earlier discoveries, and a distorted recurrence of the Jerusalem syndrome, which was associated with Paradise in his mind. He perhaps realised that his claim to the discovery of the Earthly Paradise was, at best, supra-rational, for he repeatedly said that he had come to that conclusion 'in my soul'. And he added the observation that there were probably other exploitable lands in the vicinity, which Ferdinand and Isabella could add to their empire. His new theory of the shape of the world and the location of Eden was a manifest error which his contemporaries ignored and Columbus himself repeated only once, at a time of great mental stress. Unhappily, it has helped to obscure the two great achievements which preceded it – Columbus's discovery of the variation of the Pole Star and his accurate assessment of the continental nature of the New World.

Columbus's speculations about the earthly Paradise were closely connected with the belief that his discoveries were oriental. In October 1498, he wrote to the monarchs from Hispaniola, defending this belief and the enterprise of the Indies in general against the economic and geographical arguments advanced by his critics:

> The land which God has newly given your Highnesses on this voyage must be reckoned continental in extent, wherein your Highnesses must take great joy and render Him infinite thanks and abhor them who say

that you should not spend money on this enterprise, for they are not friends of the honour of your high estate; because besides all the souls for whose salvation we can hope, whereof your Highnesses are cause, and which is our chief gain, this island alone comprises more than seven hundred leagues, and Jamaica and so great a part of the mainland [have been gained], well-known to the ancients and not unknown as the envious or ignorant say.

'Well-known to the ancients' was merely one way of saying, 'Asiatic'.

Even after Columbus had shed paradisaic fantasies for the time being, he remained understandably anxious to pursue the exploration of his latest discovery and in particular to find out its extent and exact relationship to Asia. But after his arrest by Francisco de Bobadilla and return to Spain in disgrace, the monarchs were unwilling to entrust any new enterprise to him. On his arrival in Castile in chains in October 1500, he was released but unrewarded, and left to importune the monarchs for a restoration of their favour, with payment of the revenues due to him, which had been steadily accumulating in Hispaniola, and permission to make a new voyage. But his indigence and opprobrium were unrelieved. He was allowed to present himself at Court, and the monarchs promised that he would at least recover the money due to him, though there was little prospect of his exercising again his former powers. In August 1501, according to the letters home of an Italian friend at the Spanish Court, Columbus was still 'here in disgrace, low in the favour of these monarchs, with little money'. He was obliged to witness the crushing of his expectations.

First of all, there was the continued voyaging by adventurers to his discoveries under royal licence, without his own permission or consultation, and generally without any profit to himself. We must suppose, however, that Columbus successfully revived at this time his rights to share in the costs – and therefore the recompense – of at least some of these ventures, for the monarchs at the time of his first voyage had conceded him the right to an eighth share in all transatlantic voyages, and in March 1502, Columbus wrote to inform his son that he had raised loans from the Genoese community in Seville to take advantage of this concession: 'Luis de Soria had given me all he could, and has my power of attorney ... Micer Francisco de Riverol, Micer Francisco Doria, Micer Francisco Cataño and Micer Gaspar Espindola made me loans to pay my eighth shares in the voyages of merchants who went to the Indies.'

The exploratory voyages, which angered Columbus so much, in fact

The battle between Columbus's men and the *cacique* Guarionex on the Vega Real:
natives attack the Spaniards as they try to raise a cross. From Antonio Herrera's history.

did much to extend knowledge of his discoveries and confirm suspicions
of their continental nature, while Columbus way lying impotently
in Spain, like a ship at anchor in a fair breeze. Even earlier, when
Columbus, after discovering the American mainland, was struggling
against adversity on Hispaniola, his former shipmate Alonso de Hojeda
had followed him to the coast of Paria and found the pearl fisheries that
shortly made the place renowned. Amerigo Vespucci was perhaps a
pilot on that voyage. He wrote an account of the expedition, pre-dating
it in order to make it appear earlier than Columbus's and arrogating all

Another of Herrera's views of the battle on the Vega Real.

the credit to himself. Vespucci transferred his services to Portugal and
explored much of the coast of Brazil, proving the lengthy southern
extension of the south American coast. Finally he returned to Seville
and insinuated himself into Columbus's household. He gave Columbus
the impression that he was 'a most honourable man, very desirous of
pleasing me and determined to do all he can for me', but in view of
Vespucci's falsified account of his first New World voyage, it seems
more likely that Columbus was the victim of a confidence trick. On the
basis of his widely disseminated accounts of his travels, Vespucci was

accorded the distinction of having the new continent named 'America' in his honour. In retrospect, the only element of justice in this appears to have lain in the fact that Vespucci's description of the continental nature of America and its separateness from the land-mass of the Old World, though later in date than that of Columbus, was more important than the original discoverer's in spreading knowledge of the facts. Columbus evidently did not suspect that Vespucci would rob him of renown, and his resentment against the 'Andalusian' voyagers seems to have sprung from a sense of loss of profit more than of glory.

Meanwhile, however, new and splendid Portuguese navigations were tarnishing that glory. In 1499 Vasco da Gama returned from the first European voyage to India – a feat he had accomplished by using the trade winds to make sail to the south, well into the Atlantic, before turning east and realising the old Portuguese dream of rounding the Cape of Good Hope. This voyage refurbished the probability that the shortest route to India lay round Africa, as the Portuguese had always believed, and not across the Atlantic, as Columbus had claimed. Moreover, in their next voyage to India, in 1500, the Portuguese pushed so far out into the Atlantic on the wings of the trades, that they touched Brazil. Investigation of this discovery soon proved that a considerable portion of the new continent discovered by Columbus lay in Portuguese waters, on the eastern side of the celebrated demarcation line.

Columbus was baulked not only by continuing expeditions to the zones of his admiralty and rival claims to the honour of his discovery, but also by his definitive supersession as Governor of the Indies. Bobadilla had been exercising the functions of governor since his arrival and the *coup d'état* in which he had made Columbus his prisoner, but he was not governor by title, and his office was seen essentially as investigatory and temporary. In September 1501, Ferdinand and Isabella at last made a permanent appointment in the person of Don Nicolas de Ovando, a crusty celibate of distinguished lineage, whom the monarchs had earlier made a companion of their son (to watch over his comportment). Ovando was to take up his post at Santo Domingo and govern the islands and mainland as Columbus had done, while Columbus's erstwhile colleagues Alonso de Hojeda and Vicente Yañez Pinzón, originators of the 'Andalusian' voyages, enjoyed lesser jurisdictions over parts of the mainland. Columbus still had his titles of Admiral, Viceroy and Governor, which could not be abrogated, but all substance had been stripped from them by the new appointments.

Ovando's nomination was in one respect to Columbus's advantage. Ferdinand and Isabella could now allow the Admiral to return to the

Indies without fear that he would resume power and cause further disasters by his unpopularity or incompetence. Moreover, his constant
supplications for a new voyage were having their effect, together with
the innumerable memoranda he inflicted on the sovereigns; they were
no doubt anxious to be free of his importunities in other matters, for he
would not desist from claiming restitution of his full powers and all the
sums owing to him. In March 1502, Ferdinand and Isabella therefore
approved his plan for a fourth Atlantic voyage, nearly two years after
his departure from Hispaniola in fetters. When Governor Ovando left
for the Indies in February, his fleet had numbered thirty vessels. When
Columbus followed in April, he had four caravels. He planned to
resume the explorations which the misadventures on Hispaniola had
interrupted. As Ferdinand Columbus wrote, who accompanied his
father on this voyage and whose account survives in a corrupt version,
'The Admiral's intention, as he crossed the Ocean, was to go and
reconnoitre the land of Paria.' Circumstances, however, were to dictate
otherwise.

It was known by now that the continental part of the New World,
which Columbus had discovered at Paria in 1498, occupied a large part
of the south Atlantic, but its northern extension was unknown.
Columbus believed that it would be possible to sail between the islands
he had found on his earlier crossings and this new continent through
the modern western Caribbean, where the Central American isthmus
in fact bars the way, and so reach the mainland of Asia, and the elusive
lands of gold and spices. Vasco da Gama was at the same time making
for India by his proven route to the East. If Columbus's belief were
correct, it was therefore possible that the two explorers would meet in
the Orient, having between them traversed the whole circumference of
the globe. Columbus suggested as much to the monarchs, who replied
enthusiastically:

... and with regard to what you say about Portugal we have written
appropriately to the King of Portugal, our son-in-law, and send you
herewith the letter addressed to his captain as requested by you, wherein
we notify him of his departure towards the west and say that we have
learned of his departure eastward, and that if you meet on the way you
shall treat each other as friends, and as is proper among the captains and
subjects of sovereigns between whom there is so much love and friendship and so many ties of blood, telling him that we have ordered you to
do the same; and we shall ask the King of Portugal, our son-in-law, to
write to his said captain in the same terms.

Columbus therefore hoped from this voyage for the realisation of all his frustrated ambitions, the negation of all his failures and the vindication of his successes in one crowning success. The day before his departure he wrote to the directors of the Bank of San Giorgio in Genoa, 'The things I have achieved are shining forth already and could cast a great light.' He was thinking particularly perhaps of the light of the gospel, for on the third voyage and after, he had frequently returned in his writings to the large numbers of people who would hear Christ's Word for the first time as a result of his endeavours. In preparation for the new voyage, he wrote to the Pope asking for six friars to accompany his fleet. He had been sustained in a mood of exaltation since his fall from favour and employment by scouring Scripture for texts which might constitute prophecies of great discovery. He was thus ill-prepared mentally for the disappointments that lay in wait. For this voyage, his 'High Voyage' as he called it, in which his hopes were so lofty, was to be the most manifest failure of his life; it would end not in Asia but in the depths of misery and the vicinity of despair.

The crossing of twenty-one days was the most rapid he had ever enjoyed. But there plain sailing ended. He scarcely encountered a favourable wind or current for the rest of his life. The monarchs had warned him not to disturb Ovando in Hispaniola, or even to put into that island on the outward journey 'because it is right that this voyage should not be at all delayed', though he was given permission 'when you return, God willing, if you think it necessary, to make a short stop there on the way back'. But this was not an instruction Columbus was disposed to obey. He was anxious to know how Ovando was managing his colony, and to lay claim to the moneys belonging to him which had accumulated there. Moreover, Santo Domingo was the only permanent port on that side of the ocean, and it was sensible, as well as amenable to his crew, to stop there before continuing with exploration. Moreover, when he arrived off Hispaniola, it became urgently necessary to put into port, for a hurricane was blowing up, and Columbus, who knew the ways of those waters better than anyone, accurately read the signs. He sent word to Ovando, asking to be admitted to the harbour and warning him of the oncoming storm. But the Governor ignored his request and scorned his warning. Part of the fleet that had brought Ovando from Spain set off for home in the face of the hurricane, while Columbus's vessels were forced to seek shelter in a small natural harbour he knew nearby. That night, while his flagship held fast, his other caravels broke their cables, and only by luck and daring seamanship survived. The fate of the larger fleet was a tribute to the might of the storm: nineteen ships went down with more than five than five hundred hands though a few got back to Santo Domingo. Among the dead was Francisco de Bobadilla, incarcerator of Columbus. The records of Columbus's and Bobadilla's administrations were lost, and so was the largest shipment of gold yet despatched for Spain. The only ship to make Castile was one that bore part of Columbus's own revenues, which Ovando had reluctantly released and which now would find its way into the hands of its rightful owner.

Columbus saw the hurricane as a divine intervention on his behalf and retribution on the miscreant Bobadilla. 'It has been a long time', he wrote, 'since our Lord revealed so manifest a miracle.' But his own flotilla had barely escaped. He later recalled,

> The tempest was terrible. And that night my ships broke loose and were borne off sternwards with no hope save of death; each was sure that the others were lost. Was there ever man born, without excepting Job himself, who would not have died of despair to find, in despite of my safety and my son's and brother's and friends', that at such a time the land was barred against me which by God's will I had won for Spain, sweating with blood?

The seas remained hostile and the winds contrary. Even though Columbus had come so far north in order to visit Santo Domingo, he still protested to the monarchs that he intended to sail 'to the folk of the brazil-wood' – that is, the lands he had discovered on the third voyage, the great new continent. But opposed by the southerlies, he had no option but to steer a makeshift course directly across the western Caribbean and skirt round any land he might encounter on the way. No doubt he was also reluctant to frequent the jurisdiction of Vicente Yañez and Alonso de Hojeda. He picked a course, sometimes drifting windlessly, sometimes conveyed by an unexpected current, through dangerous waters until, towards the end of July 1502, he came against the coast of British Honduras, near Bonacca at the easter end of the Bay islands. For the second time in the course of his voyages, he had stumbled on the American mainland. The new discovery threw Columbus's plans into the melting-pot once more. The coast of Honduras was continental in appearance, with an obvious hinterland of high mountains. This was confirmed by the natives, as well as by their civilised appearance, for they wore more clothing than the islanders, traded on a large scale in big, long-range canoes and worked in copper alloys. And the coast of this apparent mainland tended east-west. The question was whether this land was continuous with the continent in the south, which Columbus had discovered at Paria. If so, it would have been consistent with the explorer's earlier intentions to continue along his westward course, and look for the passage to India in that direction. But Columbus decided to turn east and sail against the wind in the direction of his former discovery.

The explanation of this conduct seems to be that Columbus was misled by information received from the natives. He understood that on the course he adopted lay a strait which led across an isthmus to a large ocean. He made at least a tentative identification in his mind of this strait with the Straits of Molucca, through which Marco Polo had travelled at the foot of the 'Golden Chersonese' or Malay Peninsula as it is now more prosaically called. If this were correct, India should lie beyond. As we know, Columbus was indeed sailing along the coast of an isthmus, and the ocean which washed it to the west was the Pacific. But the strait was non-existent, Malaya was thousands of miles away. Columbus had as yet no reliable interpreter but he had captured an Indian, now christened as 'Juan Pérez', whom he was training up for the job, but for the time being, his communications with the natives were by means of signs. Ferdinand Columbus, in his account of this voyage with his father, says that confusion arose because the native informants indicated a 'strait' or narrow strip of land – that is, the isthmus of Panama – which Columbus took to mean a strait of water 'in its more usual sense, according to his great wish'. As we have said, Columbus was made of the quintessence of wishful thinking, and his son did not fail to observe the operations of that flaw.

For nearly four months the Admiral and his men suffered the hardships, as they chased the chimerical strait, first of a gruelling beat against the wind and later, where the coast turned southwards at Cap Gracias a Dios, of a malarial coast in wretched weather and frequent torrential rain. Columbus claimed never to have witnessed weather as bad as he endured as far as Cape Gracias a Dios. The ships were damaged and the men sick; Bartolomeo Colombo's condition was gravest of all, though young Ferdinand was apparently well, while the Admiral's thoughts returned to Castile and to his elder son, Diego, 'whom I had left in Spain, orphaned and dispossessed of my honour and estate, though I was certain that there Your Highnesses, like just and grateful princes, would more than reinstate him in everything'. In Cariai – a region around the tenth parallel on the coast of modern Costa Rica – he found rumours of civilised and auriferous lands, apparently on the far coast of the isthmus. At the end of a few weeks' more unrewarding and unhealthy navigation along the coast, by late October 1502, Columbus really was in gold-bearing country, the province of Veragua, near the modern border of Costa Rica and Panama. The availability of gold was a sufficient lure to call a temporary halt in the quest for a strait. Columbus, wishful as ever, harboured hopes that this would prove his most profitable discovery so far, enrich his sovereigns and silence his detractors. But the malevolent weather would not allow him to make so great a conquest easily. Suffering from fever, like many of his men, he was driven by the gales and battered by the rain further along the inhospitable coast as far as the mouth of the Culebra River.

> There I was detained for fifteen days, by the will of the cruel weather ... I decided to postpone my intention of returning to the mines, and to do something else while awaiting weather and sea favourable for my voyage; but when I was four leagues further on the tempest returned, and exhausted me so utterly that I lost consciousness. There my wound bled some of the fever out of me. For nine days I wandered lost, without hope of survival. No eyes ever saw a sea so high, so menacing and so turned to foam. It was neither safe to run on the wind nor possible to beat against it. There I stayed in that sea of blood that bubbled like a cauldron on a great fire. No sky more terrifying was ever seen ... in all this time the downpour did not cease, and it was not so much raining as bringing down a second Flood. The crews were so oppressed that they wished for death to escape their sufferings. The ships had twice lost boats, anchors and cables and were bare and sailless.

Columbus no doubt exaggerated his tribulations, or depicted them over-vividly under the influence of fever and continuing adversity, but it was late November before he was able to begin his return to Veragua. And even then bad weather delayed his progress, so that it was not until the Feast of the Kings, 6 January 1503, that the little fleet arrived at the mouth of the river which Columbus called Belén (Bethlehem) in honour of the day. Veragua proved to be a poor return for so much suffering. At first, the signs were good: the Guaymi Indians appeared friendly and disposed, at least, to trade; moreover an expedition under Columbus's brother found rich gold deposits upriver. In fact, the gold was plentiful, but the steepness of the place and the volume of rain which falls there makes exploitation impossible (there is almost as much gold, unmined still, today as there was when Columbus found it). The Spaniards shortly experienced the deterrent effects to any would-be

1 4 9 7	1 5 0 0	1 5 0 1
Eclypsis Solis	Eclypsis lune	Eclypsis lune
29 3 2	5 14 2	2 17 49
Julij	Nouembris	Maij
Dimidia ouratio	Dimidia ouratio	Dimidia ouratio
0 36	1 37	1 52
Puncta tria	Puncta decem	

Johann Muller of Königsberg's *Calendarium* published in 1485 and containing
woodcut diagrams of the eclipses of the sun and moon from 1483 to 1530.
This sequence shows the total eclipse of the moon on 29 February 1504: Columbus
predicted this to the American Indians and thus saved the lives of himself and his
sailors on the fourth voyage.

prospectors of the torrents of water that cascade down the mountain-
sides, washing all *matériel* before them and even striking the sea and
breaking against the Spanish ships with such force that their cables
were strained or sundered. What was worse, relations with the Indians
rapidly deteriorated, as was always the case when the cupidity
and rapacity of the rank-and-file explorers was revealed. Columbus
intended to leave his brother and a garrison in a fortified post on the
banks of the River Belén, to open trade and prepare large-scale
exploitation of the gold, while the Admiral and the rest of the fleet
would take the news to Hispaniola and mount the shipment of supplies
and tools from there. But the hostile attitude adopted by the Indians,
while low water delayed the departure of the fleet, clearly jeopardised
this plan. Columbus was anxious to leave as soon as he could make
deep water, for all the ships had developed wormholes after so long
afloat in torrid waters, and he was afraid that they would not remain
seaworthy for long:

By April the ships were all worm-eaten and letting water. At about this
time a channel opened in the river mouth, through which I got out three

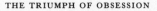

1 5 0 2	1 5 0 2	1 5 0 4
Eclypfis Solis	Eclypfis lune	Eclypfis lune
30 19 45	15 12 20	29 13 36
Septembris	Octobris	Februarij
Dimidia duratio	Dimidia duratio	Dimidia duratio
1 7	1 1	1 46
Puncta decem	Puncta tria	

of the ships, empty, with great difficulty. The boats returned to shore for salt and water. The sea rose high and menacing and would not permit the men to re-embark: the Indians were many when they fought and at last killed them. My brother and all the rest of the men were in the ship that remained in the river-mouth, and I almost alone without, on a hostile coast, with high fever and so much fatigue; the sole hope of escape was death. I climbed painfully to the top of the rigging and called with a voice of fear, weeping and in haste, for the help of Your Highnesses' captains of war, to the four quarters of the wind, but there was none to answer. Weary, I fell asleep groaning. I heard a most devout voice, 'Oh, fool, tardy to believe and serve thy God, the God of all, what more did He do for Moses and for David His servant? Since thy birth He has always kept special watch over thee. When He saw thee of an age that it pleased Him, He made they name resound marvellously in the earth. The Indies, so rich a part of the world, He gave thee for thine own. ... Turn to Him and acknowledge thy fault. His mercy is infinite. Thine old age shall not be a stumbling-block to all great deeds. ... Answer, who has afflicted thee so much and so oft – God or the world? ...

The adversity Columbus had to endure seemed all the greater now that he felt in his infirmity the onset of old age. If the gold-mining venture of Veragua failed, he had little hope of another chance in a remoter future, which death must soon curtail.

As soon as he recovered from the mental aberrations induced by his frustrations, he succeeded in embarking his brother and the short-lived garrison from their dangerous stockade before the Indians could finish them off. Columbus, as on his second voyage, had witnessed the collapse of his hopes, which brought on a temporary derangement, but from which he recovered sufficiently to extricate himself and his men from immediate danger. The problem of the worm-eaten ships' hulls, however, made any escape fraught with new danger. Their only hope was to make for Hispaniola with all speed. Pumping and bailing, they worked their way eastward along the coast on the course set by Columbus. He estimated their position accurately, with unimpaired navigational sense, and realised that they still had a considerable easting to make before getting upwind of Hispaniola, but the Admiral's prestige in the fleet can no longer have been very high, and the consensus was that their position was much further east than he estimated, and that they ought to turn away from the mainland coast as soon as possible. Perhaps the men suspected Columbus of continuing the search for a passage to India, or of attempting to establish whether the coast they were sailing was continuous with that of the land of Paria. In fact by the time they left the coast on the Darien peninsula on 1 May 1503, they had reconnoitred almost as far as the known northern extension of the continent. It therefore seemed that the mainland must indeed be continuous from Brazil to Honduras.

As Columbus had predicted, they had sought the north too soon, and their course brought them up on the coast of Cuba. A last desperate effort to reach Hispaniola, before the perforated vessels should sink, landed them short, for the wind was against them, on the Jamaican coast, at the modern St Ann's Bay. They were effectively castaways, since their ships were unusable and the nearest Spanish settlement was over 450 miles away, including more than a hundred miles of open water, at Santo Domingo. Such was the inglorious end of Columbus's 'High Voyage', and with it all his hopes of restoring his fortunes. As always in adversity, only more intensely this time, the elements of the old syndrome flowed from Columbus's distraught brain in a flood, mingled this time with the fear of old age. In Veragua, he had discovered the mines of Solomon; now he would not only recover Jerusalem, but also convert the Emperor of China to Christianity. He even repeated his claim to have discovered the Earthly Paradise.

The most disturbing feature of Columbus's mental state at this time was that he sought to circumvent the fact of his failure by senselessly affirming that he had succeeded. All the mistakes he had made and errors he had discarded, he now reasserted with the insistence that he had been right from the first. His own great achievement in realising the true nature of the American continent, and exploring its northward extension as far as Honduras was submerged beneath fallacious assertions that Cuba was a part of China, that all his discoveries were Asiatic, and that all the elements of his original theory about an Atlantic crossing, even down to the false value he assigned to the length of a degree, were right: as we have seen, while good luck made him lucid, he had transcended these mistakes to show his genius as a navigator and his deserts as a discoverer. This obstinate reversion to falsehoods that predated the evidence of his latest and most important discoveries marks the end of Columbus's intellectual development, the triumph of obsession under the influence of ill fortune. Perhaps, had Columbus not been so ruled by obsession, he would never have persevered so far as to undertake the Atlantic crossing in the first place, yet for a time, on his third voyage and perhaps for part of his fourth, he had the opportunity to shake himself free and commit his genius to the more fruitful idea, which was also his own, but which he entertained only fleetingly, of the New World's continental nature and independence of Asia.

7

THE VICTORY OF DEATH

CHRISTOFEL COLONUS.

A portrait of Columbus by Montanus: it first appeared
in *Nieuwe en Onbekende Weereld* (*The New and Unknown World*) in
1671 and is thought to have been painted in Nuremberg in
1661. This is a copy from Ogilby's *History of America* (1671).

For the time being, Columbus had to make what arrangements he could for his men's survival and rescue from their closely beached ships on the Jamaican shore. They were dependent for supplies on what they could get from the natives by truck and were restricted to a dyspeptic dies of rodents' flesh and cassava bread. When the natives became truculent and stopped the trade, Columbus showed all his resourcefulness and old ingenuity. His knowledge of the stars (so the legend goes) advised him of an imminent partial eclipse of the moon and he prefigured a hero of Rider Haggard's by using it to intimidate the Indians so that their supplies were renewed without further interruption.

His abilities were again called forth by a rebellion among a group of his own men, who conceived a plan to return to Hispaniola by canoe, but foundered and were reduced to living by terrorising the Indians. The consequences might have been disastrous for Columbus had he not finally been able to defeat the rebels in a pitched battle by the beachhead. In fact, in the meantime, Columbus had taken steps to procure the expedition's salvation. His loyal subordinate, Diego Méndez, was one of the most daring adventurers of the expedition. He had given good service in negotiations and action with the Indians in the mainland and on Jamaica but now his admiral had an even more difficult task for him. Columbus sent Méndez by canoe with Indian oarsmen to Hispaniola for help and a second canoe accompanied him, commanded by the Genoese officer Bartolomeo Fieschi. The distance was not insuperable judged by present-day standards of seamanship and endurance in small craft, but at that time the Spaniards had no experience of canoes, and to undertake the mission was a great feat of daring on Méndez's part, which he would recount with pride until his death. The severity of his passage to safety justified his vainglory. The canoe laboured against the current; the fresh water gave out; the oarsmen began to die of thirst and Méndez fell sick. At last, after five days' toiling at the oars, both canoes reached Hispaniola safely, though at a point far removed from Santo Domingo. When Columbus's men finally encountered Ovando, they found him predictably unsympathetic to the Admiral's plight. He refused to release ships for an immediate rescue, but obliged Méndez to await the next fleet from Spain and hire vessels on his own account. The consequence was that Columbus and the men who had remained with him were compelled to spend a year as castaways on their rebellious and incommodious island.

Even now, Columbus and Ovando did not appear to meet as enemies but greeted one another with professions of amity such as the monarchs expected of their servants. But Columbus departed for Spain as soon as he could. He had to endure rough passages between both Jamaica and Santo Domingo and Hispaniola and Spain, but on 7 November 1504, he finally arrived, sick, tired of contrarieties to a Castile troubled by bleak weather and a bleaker mood – for Queen Isabella was dying.

Columbus was now in his fifties and the harshness of his life had made him old before his time. His last years were to be marked by retrospectiveness, self-vindication, recrimination, concern for his posterity, and a retreat from his troubles into mysticism. This mood had been inaugurated, even before his fourth voyage, by the disappointments on Hispaniola which had followed his discovery of the mainland of the New World, culminating in his arrest and disgrace. Aboard the ship that brought him home in fetters, he wrote to Juana de Torres, who had nursed the monarchs' son, Prince John, and whose brother, Antonio, had served with Columbus in the Indies before being sent to govern the Canary Islands:

> Very virtuous lady, If my complaint against the world is a new one, its custom of ill treatment is very old. The world has met me in a thousand combats, and in all till now I resisted without the benefit of arms or counsel; cruelly, I am flung in the furnace. But hope in Him who created all sustains me. His help has always been to hand. Another time, not far off, when I was even further downcast, He raised me with His right hand, saying, 'Oh man of little faith, arise; fear not, for I am here.' I came with love so deep to serve these monarchs, and have served them with service that never was heard of or seen. Of the new heaven and earth which our Lord had made, as St John the Divine wrote after the saying from the mouth of Isaiah, He made me messenger ...

To the members of the Royal Council, he summarised his achievements in similar terms:

> My Lords, It is now seventeen years since I came to serve these monarchs in the enterprise of the Indies: the first eight were consumed in argument and in the end my opinion was taken for a matter of jest. With love I persevered and answered the French, English and Portuguese that the lands and lordships of which I spoke were for the King and Queen, my sovereigns, alone. My promises were neither few nor vain. Our redeemer ordained my path hither: there in the Indies I have brought more lands beneath His dominion that there are in Africa or Europe and

more than 1,700 islands apart from Hispaniola, which comprises more than the whole of Spain. There it is believed that the Holy Church will flourish ... In this cause I have lost my youth and the part which belongs to me of these discoveries and the glory of it – though not outside Castile, where my deeds shall be judged ... I beseech your Graces that with the zeal of true Christians in whom Their Highnesses confide so much you will examine all my writings and how I came to serve these monarchs from so far away, and left a wife and sons whom I never saw because of it, and how now, at the end of my life, I was despoiled of my honour and estate without cause, in which was respected neither justice nor mercy – not, that is to say, on Their Highnesses' part, for the blame is not theirs.

There are many inexactitudes here: Columbus's dealings with foreign powers were on his own initiative, and it was they who rejected him; he greatly exaggerates the extent of his discoveries; his account of his separation from his family is highly coloured. But all he says is true to his mood – the characteristic mood of an ageing man with a sense of failure, always looking back and apportioning blame.

The same atmosphere and imagery were sustained in the letter he sent to the monarchs from his isolation on Jamaica. He argued that no one who had opposed his enterprise should be allowed to take part in the administration of the Indies, and that even the children of his enemies should be excluded (he was perhaps thinking concretely of Alonso de Hojeda, since he went on to complain of being robbed of the pearl-fisheries). He again dilated on his own services, his sufferings in the monarchs' cause and the evangelical benefits of his work. But between 1500 and 1502 one detects one change in Columbus's writings: his mind narrowed in the only respect in which in previous years it had broadened. He returned to his old, obsessive geographical notions, such as they were before he made his great voyages, and refused to modify them even in the sense demanded by his own discoveries. Columbus could, for instance, be in no doubt that what he discovered was a continent, and in fact added an emergent mainland to his coat-of-arms, where previously only islands had been depicted, in his last years. But the southerly extension of that continent made it quite improbably that it was part of the mainland of Asia and it was almost equally improbably that so large a mainland can have existed very close to Asia, separated, for instance, only by a strait, without being known to Marco Polo. And Columbus himself had shown that the land stretched without interruptions at least as far north as Honduras. We saw how, on the third voyage, Columbus correctly assessed the nature of the American continent; even as late as his letter to Juana de Torres he was still able to write of his discovery of the mainland at Paria, 'I made a new voyage to the new Heaven and new world, which till then had remained hidden'; yet by the end of the fourth voyage, the irrational desire to vindicate himself had revivified his old obsessions. Once he had returned to them, he remained faithful to his errors to the end. In May 1505, with death drawing on, he wrote to King Ferdinand, 'Now my enterprise is beginning to open the door and I say that it is and will prove to be what I always said it was.'

When we find Columbus insisting at the end of his days that the lands he discovered were well known even before he found them 'and not unknown as the envious and ignorant say', we are surprised by the apparent paradox, which, to our way of thinking, seems to detract from the singularity of his achievement. But his meaning is clear. Columbus meant that his lands were 'known' to scholars and early travellers and to the ancients – that is, that they were Asiatic rather than antipodal, that they were, in short, as he wished them to be, and that the novelty of his enterprise consisted only in his visiting them after a long interval by a new route. In other words, from the correct assessment of his discoveries which he made on his third voyage, he had withdrawn in his closing years into an obsessive world of his own, where his own stubbornness protected him from those assaults of fortune and half-imagined enemies which had caused him so much suffering and to which he attributed the collapse of his hopes.

He also sought refuge in mysticism. Ever since the disappointments of his second voyage, Columbus had habitually worn as a penance the rough brown garb of the Franciscan brethren. This was no doubt in part a kind of inverse exhibitionism, since it would make him just as conspicuous as any admiral's finery, and penitential raiment was thought a highly commendable thing. But it was also consciously, no doubt, a genuinely religious gesture, and reflects the closeness of his associations with the Franciscans ever since the first days of friendship with Fray Antonio de Marchena and Fray Juan Pérez. Now the Franciscans harboured among their number, more than any other order, a body of esoteric mystics called 'Spirituals', under whose influence it is possible that Columbus, who was susceptible in that way, had fallen. Like Cortés after him in Mexico, he was frequently seeking to take friars to the New World rather than secular clerics, and may have intended to help them realise their ideals of a genuinely apostolic style of religion among the still unconverted and therefore uncorrupted Indians.

Certainly, millenarianism was a strong trait among these Franciscans, and we have observed many instances of the same feature in Columbus. He had always been preoccupied at moments of stress with the thought of Jerusalem and resorted often to Messianic images of David or chiliastic ones of the Day of Judgment. It is interesting that towards the close of his life he adopted a way of referring to King Ferdinand as 'Chief of the Christians', which evokes the millennial prophecies, current at the time, of the Last World Emperor. He also developed an esoteric way of signing his name, which he commanded his heirs to use but which he never explained.

The last line, for which he would sometimes substitute '*el Almirante*', we have already explained as a play on the Latin form of his name. The tripling of signs and letters perhaps represents his cult of the Holy Trinity and the last line of capitals appears to consist of the initial letters of the Holy Family. Among some spiritual millenarians, there was held to be a correspondence between the members of the Holy Family, the Persons of the Trinity and the three ages of the world, of which the last was shortly anticipated. The top two lines of the signature have been thought to represent the initial letters of some Latin motto – perhaps '*Sum Servus Altissimi Salvatoris*' ('I am a servant of the most high Saviour'), or '*Sum Sancti Adiutor Sepulchri*' ('I am an attendant at the Holy Sepulchre'), but the exact meaning of any part of the device is impossible to establish. Columbus's mysticism was also manifested in the *Book of Prophecies* he compiled chiefly from the Bible and therein principally from the prophets and psalms, in the belief that they augured his own discoveries; most of them relate to the spread of Divine revelation to new peoples, especially where islands or new lands are involved, though he made little use of the most appropriate analogy – that of Jonah, who, beckoned to the Orient, sought the havens of the West. The prophetic fashion of scriptural exegesis had become particularly strongly associated with millenarianism and mysticism through the efforts of the medieval Joachimists, whose traditions were strong in many of the Spiritual Franciscans.

The *Book of Prophecies* was only one of many literary undertakings engaged in by Columbus in his declining years. Above all, he wrote memoranda for the monarchs on questions of policy relating to the Indies, matters of navigation and his own merits, which together earned him a reputation in his own day as a voluminous scribbler. But most of his energies were consumed by writing and arguing in defence of his own financial interests in the profits of his discoveries. The mercantile spirit of his nation and family background endowed him with a material sense which his plunge into mysticism never fully submerged, yet it is probably fair to say that his material concerns were exercised more on his children's behalf than his own. He was characteristically uncompromising in pursuit of what he regarded as his financial rights, and showed no willingness in the interests of a quick return to accept a settlement that fell short of those rights. Once his revenues from the Indies began to reach him after the fourth voyage, Columbus was in fact an extremely wealthy man and though he did not have enough wealth to mount an expedition for the relief of Jerusalem, he did live in splendid style in Seville, maintaining a large household and dispensing many charitable bequests, especially in Genoa and to the shrines of his particular devotion.

The dues of which Columbus was in receipt, and which accounted for this prosperity, were principally the returns upon his own investments in mercantile transatlantic voyages, which the monarchs had permitted him to make at his discretion at the rate of 12½ per cent. We saw how between 1500 and 1502 Columbus borrowed from Genoese merchants in Seville to take advantage of this. His increments were probably now sufficient for him to make his contributions to the outgoing fleets' costs without borrowing so much from middlemen. He was also receiving the 'tenths' of the profits of trade in his admiralty, as promised to him under the Capitulations of 1492, but Columbus got only a tenth of the royal share of one-fifth, instead of the tenth of the entire sum, to which he felt he was entitled. At the end of 1504, he wrote on the back of a letter to his son Diego, 'These tenths which they give me are not what I was promised: the text of my privileges says so. And according to the terms, I am due to receive a tenth of the profits of imports and all other things, of which I get nothing.' In April 1505, King Ferdinand wrote to Governor Ovando in Santo Domingo ordering part of Columbus's tenth to be paid directly and in secret to the royal receivers of the Indies trade and revenues in Seville, so that shipping charges incurred by Columbus, presumably in the equipment of trading ventures to the New World, could be met.

The legal supplications Columbus addressed to the Crown in his last years covered not only the question of the tenth but every aspect of his fortune, including his restoration to the effective exercise of his offices and the payment of all types of revenue in his admiralty corresponding to the dues enjoyed by the Admirals of Castile in home waters. These matters remained unresolved, to be pursued after his death with as little success by Columbus's heirs. Only in 1556 did the Columbus family finally renounce the rights granted them in Capitulations of 1492 in return for new and more modest but surer revenues and the titles of dukes of Veragua, a style they still bear.

Columbus's position at Court during these supplications was greatly hampered by the sickness which had befallen the Queen. In the weeks after his return to Castile, while Isabella lay on her deathbed, Columbus received no summons to Court. The Queen and the Admiral shared almost the same age, and Columbus too was now extremely infirm and suffering still from the hardship of his fourth voyage. On 26 November 1504, the news went out that 'It has pleased our Lord to call from this life the most serene Queen, the lady Isabella.' The Admiral's reaction was coloured by his own disenchantment with life. He advised his son Diego,

It is our chief duty to commend to God most affectionately and devoutly the soul of our departed sovereign, the Queen. Her life was always catholic, virtuous and disposed to whatever might redound to His holy service; wherefore we may trust that she now rests in glory, far from all concerns of this harsh and wearisome world.

It was doubly a bad omen for Columbus. He felt his own death approaching, and he sensed the loss of his mightiest friend at Court. The new king would be Philip of Flanders, Isabella's son-in-law, who would prefer his own ministers above those supporters of Columbus whom the Queen had favoured. And pending Philip's arrival, King Ferdinand would continue to rule as regent, while men like Fonseca and Ovando, Columbus's foes, would remain in office.

The old Admiral's best hopes were in his children's future. With his bastard younger son, Ferdinand, who had turned out such a promising scholar and shown practical abilities on Columbus's fourth voyage, he was well pleased. Ferdinand had every prospect of making his way in the world. The fortunes of the house depended on the elder, legitimate and better-loved son, Diego, on whom Columbus had settled the bulk of the inheritance in 1497. Diego had distinguished himself as a courtier in the households of both the Queen and the King. Columbus relied on him as an agent at Court while he was suing for recovery of the powers and revenues he had lost, and addressed his last supplications on those scores on his son's behalf rather than his own. Diego was entitled under the terms of the Capitulations of 1492 to inherit Columbus's offices of Admiral, Viceroy and Governor, and by 1505 his father, realising he had not long to live, concentrated his efforts on stating the claims of the

heir. Diego indeed assumed those titles in due course, thought he pre-
ferred the style of Viceroy to that of Admiral, which his father had more
often employed. He made an excellent match with Maria de Toledo, of
the Duke of Alba's family, who continued the suit at Court for the
restoration of the Admiral's rights as earnestly as though she had been a
Colombo herself. In fact Diego, who had King Ferdinand's confidence,
was appointed Governor of the Indies in his own right in 1509, and
went to Hispaniola to discharge that office with distinction, so that in
some measure this part of Columbus's hopes was fulfilled albeit briefly
after his death: his son succeeded to the effective discharge of his
hereditary offices, and for a time the position Columbus had lost
returned to be enjoyed by his posterity.

In the last year of his life, Columbus disposed his affairs and brought
the threads of his career together in his will. Opening with an invoca-
tion of the Holy Trinity 'Who was mindful of me and later brought me
to perfect understanding that I should be able to sail to the Indies from
Spain', he went on to summarise the privileges the monarchs had
granted him, over which he was still arguing fruitlessly, and to recapitu-
late the discovery of Hispaniola, the cannibal lands and Jamaica. In
recalling the discovery of extensive lengths of mainland coast, he regur-
gitated the old error that he had 'discovered it on my first voyage along
with many islands' – he was thinking of Cuba, and repeating his theory
that this was Mangi, the easternmost part of continental Asia. He next
declared 'we hope in Almighty God that there shall be produced before
long a goodly and great profit in the said island and mainland, of which
... the said tenth and eighth and salaries and dues aforesaid belong to
me' and then proceeded to dispose of these largely non-existent sums.
He was betraying his wishful thinking again. It was most unlikely that
the monarchs' old promises would ever be fulfilled in the sense in which
Columbus interpreted them, or with the generosity he seems to have
expected.

After establishing the order of succession of his heirs, he ordered all
future heads of his house to adopt the mysterious signature we
described above. He designated Diego heir to his offices, and ordered
him to provide for the other members of the family from the estate. He
assigned part of the inheritance for the maintenance of a branch of the
family in proper style in Genoa, so that his links with his native city
should never be severed. A deposit was to be made in the San Giorgio
Bank against the day when his successors should be able to fulfil his
promise and liberate Jerusalem 'so that interest shall accumulate until
the day when some good work can be achieved in this matter of

Jerusalem, for I believe that once the King and Queen, our sovereigns and their successors set their determination on it, their Highnesses will be moved to accomplish it, or will provide aid and material to the servant and vassal who shall do so in their name'.

He further charged his successors to insist on their rights to his presumed revenues from the Indies, saying that he reckoned his own dues at twenty-five per cent of the profits (he was receiving only a tenth of the royal fifth, or a total of two per cent). His heirs were always to resist heresy and schism in the Church, and to serve the rightful Pope in any such eventuality. They were 'to work always for the honour and good and increase of the city of Genoa', saving only their prior duty to the Church and to the kings and queens of Spain. Columbus next ordered a church and hospital to be founded on Hispaniola, dedicated to the Virgin of the Conception, where Masses should be said in the chapel for the salvation of his soul. Furthermore, four good teachers of Divinity were to be maintained on the island to instruct the Indians, and as the income from the inheritance should increase, his heirs were to spend correspondingly more on the work of converting the natives 'and for this let there be no grief in spending all that may be necessary'.

Columbus had never recovered from the agues he contracted on his fourth voyage. For years now those once-famous vermeil locks had been quite white and then, in the final months of life, that body that had travelled so far was unable to move. His disappointments had disposed him to die. On 20 May 1506, after ratifying the terms of his testament and receiving the last rites, he committed his soul to the Lord to Whom he had dedicated his voyages.

That a weaver's son had died titular Admiral, Viceroy, Governor and nominal Counsellor of the King of Spain constituted a great personal achievement. But Columbus's greatness must be judged by his contribution to mankind, not his accomplishments for himself. His contemporaries had a mixed view of that contribution. The New World did not come to play a full part in the history of the Old for some two hundred years, and other explorations – especially those of Vasco da Gama and Magellan – seemed in the short term more important economically. But the sheer extent of the new lands across the Atlantic, and the large numbers of new peoples brought within hearing of God's word, left men with little doubt of the potential importance of the events connected with Columbus's life. By 1552, the historian López de Gómara could characterise the discovery of the New World as the greatest happening since the incarnation of Christ. Yet the same writer denied that

Columbus was truly the discoverer of those lands. This was a representative sentiment. Columbus had complained even in his own lifetime of being 'despoiled of the honour of his discovery', and though he perhaps referred to the stintedness of his acclaim rather than to any denials of the pertinent fact, it is true that his reputation has since suffered repeatedly from attempts to attribute the discovery of the New World to someone else.

The early history of the controversy was dominated by the legal wrangle between Columbus's heirs and the monarchs of Spain over the non-fulfilment of the royal promises of 1492. Witnesses were procured to support the Crown's case by asserting that Columbus had not kept his side of the bargain. It was said, for instance, that the credit for the discovery Columbus undertook to make belonged to Martín Pinzón, or that it rested with an 'unknown pilot' who had preceded Columbus to the New World by chance and confided his knowledge to the Genoese when on the point of death. It was this last story which López de Gómara repeated, and it has been echoed ever since. Testimony was even obtained – almost certainly not without deliberate perjury – to deny the undoubted fact that Columbus had visited the American mainland on his third voyage. The discoverer's sons, Diego and Ferdinand, strenuously resisted these allegations. Diego had the testimony of numerous witnesses recorded on his father's side and Ferdinand wrote extensively in defence of his claims. It must be said that whatever Martín Pinzón's role on the first transatlantic voyage, of which we shall never know the whole truth, he joined the enterprise only at a late stage, when Columbus's plans were already well advanced. Though Columbus was familiar with many mariners' tales of unknown lands in the west, the story of the unknown pilot is unacceptable as it stands, firstly because it is technically impossible to cross the Atlantic 'by accident' – the necessary winds were not strong enough nor long enough sustained – and also because, as we know, he had obtained sufficient evidence of lands in the west by his own researches, without necessary recourse to unknown mariners. The presumed mariner can anyway not have helped Columbus very much, since his information was evidently insufficient to dispel Columbus's belief that his discoveries were Asiatic. The admiral's doubts on that score, when they arose, were clearly attributable to his own observations.

Columbus's rivals soon multiplied when Vespucci's accounts of his voyages became known. There is no doubt that Vespucci's claim to have visited the continental part of the New World before Columbus rests on the falsely pre-dated relation of his adventure with Alonso de

Hojeda in the Gulf of Paria. In fact, Columbus had preceded them in those lands by several months. Vespucci's modern admirers place more emphasis on the allegation that the Venetian was first to perceive the true nature of America as a continent separate from the Eurasian land-mass. But, as we have argued, Columbus has the prior claim in this respect too, and if Columbus's opinion wavered, no more was Vespucci's unequivocal or unchanging. Only a year after Columbus's death, Martin Waldesmüller proposed that the new continent be named in honour of Amerigo Vespucci, whom he proclaimed a geographer equal to Ptolemy. Not long after, the same distinction was urged on Vespucci's name by the Academy of Lyons. It is pointless to say that 'America' is a misnomer, but it is important to realise that the name is owed not to any genuine prior claim on Vespucci's part to a discovery which truly belongs to Columbus, but to the chance whereby the Venetian was more effective in spreading knowledge of the discovery and of its true nature that the Genoese.

Recent historians have added to Columbus's rivals by adducing Norsemen from proto-historical sagas or even early Welshmen and Hibernians from remoter and more misty myths. It is acceptable that the Vikings, at least, touched America in the course of their navigations, but their random voyages and current-driven errantry are not comparable with the consciously exploratory travels of Columbus. It does not seem that the Vikings were effective in increasing man's geographical knowledge as Columbus was, for almost all record of their encounter or encounters with the American mainland soon disappeared or was preserved only in folk memory. The only evidence that any scientific significance was attached to the saga tradition of a Viking presence in America lies in the so-called 'Vinland Map', which some scholars have supposed to be a genuine cartographical product of the mid-fifteenth century: the map apparently depicts part of North America in the form of an island named 'Vinlandia' – the Norse name for the western land of the saga tradition. Unfortunately for those who believe in the authenticity of the map, the depiction of the North American coast is not the only respect in which it is an anomalous or anachronistic document, compared with other products of its supposed time. This, combined with a mystifying obscurity which surrounds the origins of the map, arouses a strong presumption that it is merely a clever modern forgery. In any case, the 'Vinland Map' is isolated from the mainstream of medieval geographical science, and cannot be said to affect Columbus's achievement.

An alternative argument, still connected with the Norsemen, but voiced more often by admirers of Vespucci, is that Columbus's discovery of America was no better than that of the Vikings, since he came upon the New World quite haphazardly and failed to identify it correctly. It has also been said that neither Columbus nor anyone up to his time anticipated the possibility of a second world land-mass being found, and that it is imprecise to speak of the 'discovery' of something which the European mind was not pre-disposed to comprehend. Rather, the discovery of America happened gradually and cumulatively, as, under the influence of further explorations, men's presuppositions became adapted to the facts. Now it is agreed that one cannot be said to have 'discovered' a thing without knowing what it is one is supposed to have discovered – otherwise the event is a mere accident, which will pass unnoticed unless someone else happens to make the identification which the finder failed to make. Such was not the case, however, when Columbus discovered America.

We have tried to show in the first place, that the possibilities of just such a discovery as Columbus made – that of a continent separate from the known Eurasian land-mass – were suspected and actively canvassed among scholars prior to Columbus's departure under the name of 'the Antipodes'. Secondly, we have suggested that Columbus on his third voyage correctly identified the mainland he discovered with this rumoured continent. During the derangement brought on by his subsequent sufferings, Columbus foresook the idea, and even while he still embraced it, his opinion of the proximity of his discoveries to Asia was grossly exaggerated. But he was nonetheless the first man correctly to assess the nature of the New World, in an opinion which, thanks to his sons and in the longer term to Las Casas, became known in his day or shortly after.

Despite four hundred and fifty years of assiduous detraction, his prior role in the discovery of America remains the strongest part of Columbus's credentials as a great explorer. On the other hand, it is right to see the discovery of America as a long historical process, which began with Columbus but continued to unfold bit by bit after his time, rapidly at first and then more slowly. Within a few years of Columbus's death a general picture of the true nature of the New World had been clearly expressed and became widely known, but it was still only a matter of probabilities. On the main point at issue, for instance, between Columbus and his geographical adversaries, the historian Fernández de Oviedo was obliged to point out as late as 1535 that the exact relationship of America to Asia was still unknown. Not until the end of the century was their separateness one from the other proven. It was a matter of several generations after Columbus before a reasonably accurate and comprehensive description of America was possible, and even today parts of that vast continent remain imperfectly explored.

We have seen how despite the deficiencies of his education, Columbus attained the highest importance in the history of science. His servility before old texts, combined with his paradoxical delight when from his own experience he was able to correct them, marks him out at once as one of the last torch-bearers of the Middle Ages, who carried their lights on the shoulders of their predecessors, and one of the first beacons of the Scientific Revolution, whose glow was kindled from within by their preference for experiment over authority. The same sort of paradox enlivened every aspect of his character. His attraction towards fantasy and wishful thinking was ill accommodated in that hard head, half-full already with a sense of trade and profit. In his legal relations with the Crown and concern for his posterity, his mysticism was tempered by a materialism only slightly less intense. Though religion was a powerful influence in his life, its effects were strangely limited: despite his zeal to convert the Indians, for instance, he could also behave callously towards them. He was untruthful, without being mendacious. He was proud of his humble origins, but still anxious for ennoblement. He loved adventure, yet could not bear adversity. Most paradoxically of all, beyond the islands and mainlands of the ocean, Columbus explored involuntarily the marchlands between genius and insanity. Times of stress habitually deranged him; in his last such sickness, he obsessively discarded his own latest and most luminous ideas, and never fully recovered.

It probably helped to be a visionary, with a flair for the fantastic, to achieve what he achieved. The task he set himself – to cross the Ocean Sea directly from Europe to Asia – was literally beyond the capacity of any vessel of his day. The task he performed – to cross the ocean from Europe to the New World – was beyond the conception of many of his contemporaries. To have accomplished the highly improbable was insufficient for Columbus – he had wanted to conquer the impossible. He died a magnificent failure: he had not reached the Orient. His failure enshrined a greater success: the discovery of America.

One cannot do him justice without making allowances for the weakness that incapacitated him for ill fortune. On his second and third voyages, it was only because in his heart he acknowledged the truth – that Cuba was an island or Paria an unknown continent and neither part of Asia – that he sought refuge from the consequences of failure by trying to mask the facts. In a sense, the fervour with which in his last years he insisted on the Asiatic nature of his discoveries is proof that he had once realised his mistake: it was characteristic of him to abjure his achievement in discovering a new continent, because he could not face failure in the attempt to reach an old one. He wanted to repeat his boast, 'When I set out upon this enterprise, they all said it was impossible', without having to admit that 'they' were right.

Further Reading

S.E.Morison, *Admiral of the Ocean Sea* (Boston, 1942) is one excellent English life of Columbus among many bad ones. See also W.D. and C.R.Phillips, *The Worlds of Christopher Columbus* (Cambridge, 1992) and F. Fernández-Armesto, *Columbus* (London, 1996).

On various aspects of the background, see:

C.R.Beazley, *The Dawn of Modern Geography* (Oxford, 1896–1906)

F. Fernández-Armesto, ed., *The Times Atlas of World Exploration* (London, 1991)

V.I.J.Flint, *The Imaginative Landscape of Christopher Columbus* (Princeton, 1992)

G.E.Nunn, *Geographical Conceptions of Columbus* (New York, 1924)

E. O'Gorman, *The Invention of America* (Bloomington, 1961) – this should be compared with the rejoinder by Marcel Battaillon, translated in J.R.L. Highfield (ed.), *Spain in the Fifteenth Century* (London, 1971)

L. Olschki, 'What Columbus Saw', *Proceedings of the American Philosophical Society*, lxxxiv (1941), 633–59

J.H.Parry, *The Age of Reconnaissance* (London, 1963)

R.Pike, *Enterprise and Adventure* (New York, 1966)

C.O.Sauer, *The Early Spanish Main* (Berkeley, 1965)

E.G.R.Taylor, *The Haven-finding Art* (London, 1956)

J.O.Thomson, *History of Ancient Geography* (Cambridge, 1948)

L.De Vorsey and J. Parker, *In the Wake of Columbus* (Detroit, 1985)

I translate a selection of documents in F. Fernández-Armesto, *Columbus on Himself* (London, 1991). A picturesque old translation of Peter Martyr's *De Orbe Novo* by Richard Eden is in E. Arber (ed.), *The First Three English Books on America* (Birmingham, 1885). The translations in this book from Dr Chanca's letter are based on Ybarra's in *Smithsonian Collections*, xlviii (1907).

INDEX